Decorative 6" Quilt Blocks

Catherine H. Anthony

DOVER PUBLICATIONS, INC.
Mineola, New York

All photographs by Jim Anthony except "Turn About" shown on inside back cover, which was photographed by Birlauf and Steen of Denver, Colorado.

Copyright

Copyright © 1983 by Catherine H. Anthony.
All rights reserved under Pan American and International Copyright Conventions.

Published in Canada by General Publishing Company, Ltd., 30 Lesmill Road, Don Mills, Toronto, Ontario.
Published in the United Kingdom by Constable and Company, Ltd., 3 The Lanchesters, 162–164 Fulham Palace Road, London W6 9ER.

Bibliographical Note

Decorative 6" Quilt Blocks, published by Dover Publications, Inc. in 1997, is a republication of *Sampler Supreme: Showcase Quilt for the Six-Inch Pieced Block*, originally published by Leone Publishing Co., Santa Clara, CA in 1983. The original color section has been omitted; some of the color photos are now shown on the covers of the book.

Library of Congress Cataloging-in-Publication Data

Anthony, Catherine H.
    [Sampler supreme]
    Decorative 6" quilt blocks / Catherine H. Anthony.
        p.   cm.
    Originally published: Sampler supreme. Santa Clara, CA: Leone Pub. Co., 1983.
    Includes bibliographical references.
    ISBN 0-486-29674-1 (pbk.)
    1. Patchwork—Patterns. 2. Quilting—Patterns. 3. Patchwork quilts. I. Title.
TT835.A54 1997
746.46'041—dc21
                                     97–6512
                                     CIP

Manufactured in the United States of America
Dover Publications, Inc., 31 East 2nd Street, Mineola, N.Y. 11501

Acknowledgments

I salute each maker of every quilt I have ever seen and loved. A special tribute to my first quilting teacher, Mary Woodard Davis, who has been a continuing friend and influence for the past twelve years. Without the love and assistance of my daughter Libby Lehman, this book would not have been written. Her talents in artwork, designing, and drafting are very appreciated. Thanks and kisses to my photographer, adviser, and husband, Jim Anthony. Bouquets to Diana Leone for her patience, prodding, and publishing expertise. My gratitude to my employees at the Quilt Patch for their encouragement and consideration. Thanks to Jack McCaine for drafting some of the patterns. Garlands of praise for these special teachers whose quilts, classes, books, and friendship have so influenced my work: Jinny Beyer, Nancy Crow, Chris Edmonds, Jeffrey Gutcheon, Nancy Halpern, Michael James, Jean Ray Laury, Bonnie Leman, Diana Leone, and Marjorie Puckett. To my students, who are the makers of the quilts pictured in this book, a thanks from everyone for letting us enjoy them. And to each of my students I send love for sharing a part of their life and work.

Contents

Introduction

This book offers a variety of six-inch pieced blocks that can be used to create a sampler quilt showcasing your quiltmaking talents. The book is for those quiltmakers who relish the challenge of intricate patterns requiring precise piecing and ingenious use of fabric to reach the full perfection of the pieced quilt. Such a quiltmaker would be considered past the beginner stage. Therefore the instructions and suggestions are meant as additions to previous knowledge of basic quiltmaking. Each of the 6" patterns is a symmetrical design and may be used set square or on the diagonal. Full-size grids facilitate drafting other traditional patterns or original designs. The scale of the quilt in relation to the six-inch block is very important. The beauty of the individual blocks should not be lost in the sheer bulk of a great many blocks sewed in one quilt. As few as four or five blocks set together and enhanced with borders can be beautiful. Choose your patterns and let the quilt reflect your skills, ideas, and style. Make it like you want to; make it distinctly *yours!*

Getting Started

The best way to get started is simply to begin. However it is more fun to begin with something you like; a color, a design, a pattern, or a special place for the quilt to be used. Having made one decision, others will begin to fall in line with the first. And you are already started. Don't be inflexible with decisions. Leave room for changes, additions, deletions, surprises, and more changes.

To do fine work you must use the best materials and tools that are available to you. They need not be the most expensive, but everything should be of good quality and in good working order. This is in keeping with the traditions of our quilting grandmothers. Often scraps were all that was available to them, but they saved the best for "fine work" and used the rest for "kivers."

Since this book and the quilts discussed are for the quiltmaker with some experience, no supply list will be given. Every quiltmaker has her own favorite tools and ways of doing things. If what you are doing works, it is the right way for you, although you will probably constantly search for improvements in your methods. In here I discuss some of the ways I have found to work well in designing and executing six-inch blocks in a sampler quilt. If a special tool is used or needed, I mention it as part of the method being discussed.

Templates

After selecting a pattern, you must make the templates. **Utmost accuracy in your templates is vital.** In such small pieces as used in six-inch blocks, even a very small error is in fact a large one. Plastic template material is much preferred. Plastic is more accurate, durable, and you can see through it to use the print of the fabric as you design your patterns. Plastic template material is available in most quilt shops and from many of the mail-order sources advertised in quilt magazines.

A "Pilot" brand "ultrafine point permanent SU-UF" pen should be used to mark on the plastic. These pens are available where office, school or art supplies are sold.

Cut your plastic into a useable size (not over 6″ square). Place the plastic over the pattern design piece. To keep it from shifting as you work, hold it in place on the pattern page by taping lightly with masking tape across two corners of the plastic. Mark points of the pattern piece with dots. Using a ruler (except on curves), draw lines between the dots. Label the piece with the pattern name and block size. Because of the small size, you may have to abbreviate.

Remove the tape and carefully cut out the template. You may cut on or along the line, but be consistent and cut every template in exactly the same way. Check your template's accuracy by placing it over the pattern. If there's any variance, discard that template and make another one.

These small templates can be taped (with transparent tape) to a colored index card marked with the name and size of the pattern. The colored card makes it easy to find.

A small "Ziploc"® storage bag may be stapled, on the four corners, to a notebook divider page. This makes an excellent storage place for the index card with templates taped to it. The bag also has room for the pattern drawing or design notes. Another bag for another pattern may be stapled to the back side of the notebook divider page.

"Joining Marks"

A whole piece is sometimes sewed to a pieced section. The point where seams of the pieced section join the whole piece should be marked on the template.

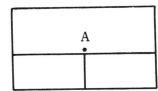
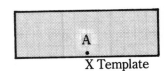

A is the "joining mark"

X Template

When the sewing lines for template "X" are marked on the fabric, the "joining mark" should be marked in the seam allowance of the fabric. When piecing and sewing, this "joining mark" will show the proper location for the seam of the pieced section.

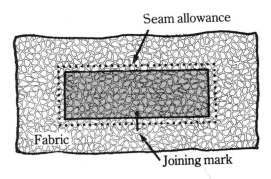

Seam allowance

Fabric

Joining mark

Sometimes "joining marks" are made on longer pieces to assure proper position. This is especially helpful if the edge of the piece is cut on the bias of the fabric. "Joining marks" should be on both templates of longer pieces.

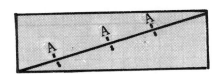

All curved-seam templates should have "joining marks" to assure proper fit.

Precision Piecing

Accurate drafting, exact marking, and precise cutting are all requirements for precision piecing. If any of these requirements is faulty, even skilled piecing cannot overcome the fault. So do it exactly right from the very first.

When fabric pieces have been cut, they should be pinned in the correct pattern position on a piece of fabric. A twelve-inch square of muslin, pellon, or flannel works very well for this. Then, no matter how long before the pieces are sewed together, the planned design, layout, and pieces will not be lost. The "pin-up" can be folded and put in a plastic "Ziploc®" bag, handy for carrying in your purse or sewing basket.

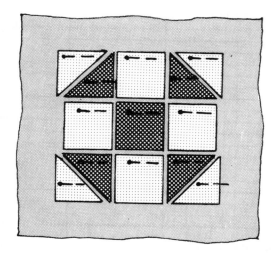

The six-inch block uses the customary ¼" seam allowances—except with small pieces (less than ⅜" square) where larger seam allowances should be used to facilitate handling. After sewing, any extra seam allowance should be trimmed away.

Where many seams come together, creating bulk, some of the ¼" seam allowance may be trimmed **after** the pieces have been sewn together. Sometimes it will be advisable to trim the finished seams of the block to make quilting easier. However, you should consider how the quilt will be used because the trimmed seams are not as strong.

Needles should be fine and as small as you can skillfully use. I recommend a #9,10, or 12 "between." Discard any bent, rusty, or snagged needles. If threading is a problem, buy a package of needle threaders. The ones from Japan are fragile but will go in tiny needles. Discipline yourself to thread several needles at once; an "already threaded needle" is such a luxury!

Pins should be very fine, sharp, and as slim as a needle. In fact, if you don't have good pins, use some of your small needles as pins. The heads of the pins should be small with no beads. The weight of the beaded pins is too much for the tiny pieces. Pins labeled "extra fine pleating pins" are very good. Too coarse or too heavy a pin will distort the sewing lines and throw off the piecing.

You will need a good pair of sharp scissors with sharp points to cut and trim seam allowances and to clip thread. Large dressmaker shears are too cumbersome for precise work. A really good pair of scissors should last for years if you take care of them—and keep them hidden from everyone else!

The color of the thread is very important. It should match the fabric colors as closely as possible. General rules for color of thread:

- when sewing black and white, use black thread

- when sewing a light and dark, use matching dark

- when sewing a print and a solid, match the solid

- when sewing two prints, match something the prints have in common (for example, green leaf or black, squiggly line)

- when in doubt, try a medium-dark gray.

Medium-dark gray thread blends well with many colors. Try it. Lay a medium-dark gray thread across an assortment of colored fabrics. Then try white thread. Then try natural-colored thread. Then try any color you think will work better. The gray thread usually blends with more of the colors than any of the other thread.

Since most quilts made of the six-inch block are usually for "show" instead of hard use, a finer denier thread works very well. This finer thread makes a "less stiff" seam and it pulls smoothly through the fabric without knotting or tugging. Such thread is made by several companies and is usually labeled "Extra fine for light weight fabrics and machine embroidery." It is cotton-covered polyester. J&P Coats Dual Duty Plus, and Mettler Silk Finish are the brands available to me. If you compare a strand of this thread with a strand of regular mercerized cotton thread, you will see that the mercerized is thicker and coarser.

Don't say, "The color of thread doesn't matter; it won't show." **It will show. Inevitably.** And you need everything working for you.

After the block is pieced, press the whole block. (Again, ironing on a towel helps.) How much you press while piecing is up to you. A finished block should be kept unfolded. Two seven-inch pieces of cardboard taped to form "a book" make a good case for keeping finished six-inch blocks.

Pinning and Sewing

It is extremely important to sew **exactly** on the marked sewing lines! Start by matching the end points of the seam you are going to sew; insert a pin into the end point marked on one piece, then through the point on the other piece. Just put the pin about half way through, not pushed in all the way. It should stick up like a little flagpole and should not lay flat against the material. **Leave it this way.** If you push the pin in all the way or try to pin "along" the seam, you distort the seam and cannot sew it perfectly straight.

In a similar manner, you should also pin any joining marks (the marks where the end point of one piece joins the other piece somewhere along the seam line, or marks made in the middle of both seam lines) especially on curved seams. Again, insert a pin through the joining mark on one piece, then through the mark on the other piece. Be very careful and do this very accurately. Since seams are short, there should not be more than three or four pins per seam.

If a pin misses the mark on either piece—even slightly—take it out and do it right. With pieces this tiny, even a small error is disastrous!

Sew the seam by taking small, even stitches **exactly** on the marked sewing line. Use a short length of thread (about 12" to 18"). Insert the needle through the starting points marked on both pieces. Get several stitches on the needle, then flip the fabric over to make sure the stitches are exactly along the seam line of the bottom piece. If not, remove the needle and try again. When stitches are exactly on both seam lines, pull the thread on through and repeat the procedure. Remove pins as you approach them. Do **not** try to sew around them.

Keep checking to make sure stitches are on both seam lines. It is much easier to pull out a needle and try again than to pull out thread already sewn in place. Take several back stitches along each seam. Sew only to the end points marked on both pieces, then knot thread to end the seam. Never sew past the seam end point, and never sew down the seam allowance material. When sewing across a previously sewn seam, sew up to the seam allowance. Then pass the needle through the end points only. Then continue on the other side.

Precise pinning is also essential when you begin to piece sections of the block together. As each section is made up of pieces already sewn together, you must take extra care to make sure the seams of both sections line up exactly where they should in the finished block. The sections should be pinned together through the end points and then through any intersecting seams. In pinning be sure to catch a few threads of each fabric at the intersecting points of the two seams. When sewing, again catch a thread or two of each fabric at the intersection.

When many seams come together at a common point—such as the center of a star—sew the pieces into two equal sections, or halves of the star.

Precision Piecing

At the center of each section, where all the seams meet, make a small stay stitch in the seam allowance to stabilize all the points. In each half, press all seam allowances in the same direction. The direction may be determined by the color of pieces. If a very light colored piece is next to a very dark piece, press the seam allowance toward the dark piece so it will not show through the light piece. When all the seams are pressed, look at the right side of the section. One piece will appear to lay "on top" of the others. This piece will now be called "piece A."

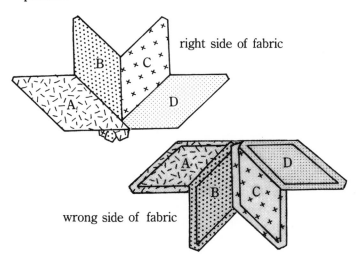

right side of fabric

wrong side of fabric

On the wrong side of one half, insert a pin through the end point of piece D. Turn the fabric over, and make sure the pin catches a thread or two of piece A. Now, on the other half, make sure the pin catches a few threads on the right side of piece A, then continues through the end of piece D. The pin should remain sticking up and down just like described above for joining small pieces.

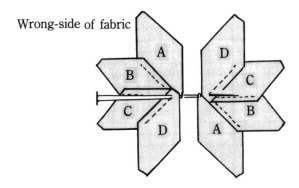

Wrong-side of fabric

Sew the two sections together making sure to sew precisely on the marked seam lines of both sections. Back stitch frequently. Sew up to the center where you have pinned. Take a tiny back stitch right next to the center point. Insert the needle through the lifted seam allowances. Take a stitch and a tiny back stitch immediately past the center point. Continue to sew the rest of the seam.

Take care in pressing. Points that meet perfectly can be distorted with the iron. To minimize distortion, spread a hand towel out flat on top of the ironing board. If you are ironing a bulky seam, iron the fabric right side up.

Use of Fabric and Color

Choosing your fabric

Color

The first thing you see in a quilt is the color, then the design, and then the workmanship. The most important thing about the color is that it pleases you. You will only do your best work on something you really like.

However, there are many ways to make colors work together and enhance each other. Some of the best uses and theories of color specifically for quiltmakers are in Michael James' *The Second Quiltmaker's Handbook* and Jeffrey Gutcheon's *Diamond Patchwork.*

Part of the joy of the six-inch block is that it allows you to use really dashing color in small amounts without having it overpower everything else.

To see how this works, find a fabric in a color you really like, and use this as a starting base. Then choose fabrics of a lighter and a darker shade of the background color of the favorite fabric. Are there any accent colors in the fabric? Find other fabrics that can complement that accent; often you will find a muted shade of the accent color. For example, if the fabric has an accent of a little flower of bright yellow, put a fabric of a muted yellow and a matching bright yellow fabric next to the favorite fabric. The matching bright yellow often overpowers the favorite fabric, while the muted yellow enhances or even makes the little yellow flower seem brighter and larger. When seeking yellows, look to the khakis, tans, and beiges; they often appear very yellow when worked in with prints.

You will need a very dark-colored fabric to give your piece depth and importance. Instead of dulling colors, black has a way of sharpening and defining other colors. If black seems too much, use colors that are almost black (but not bright) such as Hunter green, Navy blue, antique red, maroon, dark chocolate brown, deep purple, or charcoal. Without this depth of color, a certain enduring richness will be lost.

Hang one of your quilts that you like on the wall. Stand back from it, and squint hard as you look at it. What do you see first? What stands out the most? It is the very lightest colors! Did you mean for them to stand out that much? ... to be the most important? Many who would never use even a dash of black will use muslin, white, light pink or yellow with free abandon! True, the "lights" are very important for they lend contrast to the other colors. But plan their use as "special" and they can be wonderful highlights. In a sampler quilt, place the blocks with strong "lights" so they are balanced and not concentrated in one part of the quilt.

Now for the unexpected. The "zinger." This is color used much as you would put paprika on an egg for spice or flavor. If most of your colors are muted prints, try a bright or light solid. If most of your colors are pastel, try a deep bright shade of one of the pastels. Experiment. Remember that you will be using only small amounts, so while the whole bolt seems outlandish, a ½" piece might be just right.

Do the fabric colors you have selected seem heavy? Do these colors need some "space" in them? Try adding "sky color" in with other colors. Many shades of gray, blue or mauve classify as "sky colors." Look outside; all sky is not bright blue. Nancy Halpern is especially talented in using such "space" in her quilts. This use of a neutral space color with your other colors will have the effect of freeing or easing the colors used in your pattern designs. White, natural, or pale beige might give the appearance of space, but they can also appear to be "blank" or create a void. A very light color in the center of a pattern can appear as a hole in the design.

If your colors seem to need something to pull them together or level them out, do as nature does—try a bit of brown or some green. Select several shades of the color to see which will work best. Such an addition will sometimes give the color combination a more natural and less contrived look.

Matching a color perfectly is not always possible, nor is it always the best solution. Try two shades, one lighter and one darker than the desired match, and use them both. Or do a gradation of the color through several shades from light to dark. This can sometimes be overdone as in monochromatic (all one color) schemes, which are always safe but often dull. To be successful, there must be a high degree of contrast between the lights and darks. In a color gradation, the fabrics don't all have to be a solid color; you can mix in some prints.

There are no rules about the number of different colors. Have enough coordinating colors so there is blending, contrast, reinforcement, interest, and excitement; but don't have so many as to be confusing.

Yardage

There are many similarities between an artist's paints and a quiltmaker's fabrics. An artist does not paint a tree from one tube of green for leaves, a tube of brown for the trunk, and a tube of blue for the sky. She will have several shades of green, brown, and blue plus some white for tints, black for shading, yellow for highlights, pinks and reds for warmth, and her favorite color that always goes with everything. What's more, she is not expected to use every smidgeon of every tube of paint! A quiltmaker needs a palette of fabrics of various colors and sizes of prints. Like the artist, there should be no "guilts" about not using up the last inch of fabric. And that is my statement about yardage!

Fabric Content:

Fabrics of 100% cotton are a must for working with the size pieces in the six-inch block. Fabrics of blends of cotton and man-made fibers require larger seam allowances than are feasible with such small pieces. All fabrics should be washed and pressed before using. This is done to remove any excess dye and take care of shrinkage. Medium-weight or light-weight dress fabrics work best. Even slightly heavier or thicker fabrics cause problems of bulk. Sleazy, gauzy, or fragile fabrics ravel and will not hold their cut shape. Remember that you need everything working for you and not against you. A quilt made from fabrics with a difference in the sizes of prints is usually more interesting. Most new quiltmakers think all quilts are made using allover prints. With experience and exposure to many quilts, the eye begins to perceive the nuances, movement, and accents that a variation in the scale of prints can give to a quilt. Know-how in mixing prints takes some trial-and-error, but that's half the fun.

In a sampler quilt there are many different designs, and some unity is desired so that the quilt doesn't look like a hodge-podge. Color can be one unifying force, especially if one fabric is used as a background in the blocks. Some or all of the pieces along or around the outside of each block are all of the same fabric. It is most important that all the corners of the blocks be of the same fabric. Avoid using any of the sashing fabric in the corners or outside pieces.

Prints

Small allover prints and tone-on-tone prints of one color can be used almost interchangeably with solids. Back off six to eight feet from the fabric and see if it looks like a solid from that distance. If so, it will work. And the print viewed up close will yield an added surprise. Sometimes small prints can have a spotty appearance, even when viewed from a distance. Avoid them.

Allover prints of a somewhat larger scale work well, especially if there is an "intertwining" effect. This tends to keep the eye moving and interested.

Medium, large and "really large" prints are often overlooked by the quiltmaker. This is a shame and a loss. One large flower or leaf might give several shades of color for small pieces, while the space between the large flowers gives a matching solid! Equally intriguing can be the very busy paisley prints. Pieces cut showing wonderful curls and wavy lines can make a pattern take on a new dimension.

Stripes are wonderful! They lead the eye in the direction and movement of the design. Stripes don't have to be all solid lines; they can be dots, dashes, wavy lines, garlands, prints, solids, and all sorts of mixtures. Usually challenging, they almost always add to the dimension in a design. If you don't add at least one stripe into your fabric collection for your sampler, you and the quilt will be missing something.

Solid color fabrics have very valid uses when mixed in with prints. A solid color fabric gives a definite design "line." The exact shape of the pattern piece is immediately and definitely defined. With prints the exact shape of the pattern piece may be vague or almost lost, depending upon the print or the template placement on the print.

Use of Fabric

Where you place the template on the printed fabric makes or changes your block design. This is especially important in the special or featured print, the larger prints, and stripes. For example, here's a fabric with a special flower used different ways in a simple four-patch to go somewhere in the block.

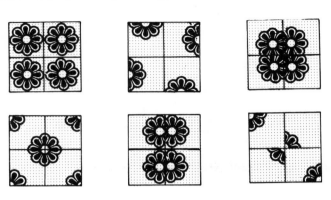

Each uses the same-sized piece of the same fabric, but the design effect is different. One is not better than any of the others, but the way the four-patch looks in the total block design will be different. Other shapes also have different possibilities.

Utilize the "space" between the flowers.

Diamonds

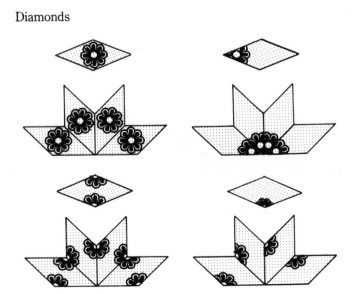

You are now designing with the color, the shape of the block piece, and the prints on the fabric.

Use of Fabric—Prints

To make sure your fabric is cut where you want your featured "flower" to appear, you must use a plastic template material that you can see through, and a permanent, fine-point marking pen to mark on the plastic. The plastic may be clear or frosted.

1. With fabric right-side up, place plastic template over featured "flower" on fabric. Locate "flower" exactly where you want it to appear. With the permanent pen, draw the simple outline of "flower" on plastic.

2. Write "UP" on face of template where you have drawn the flower.

3. Turn fabric wrong-side up. Turn template over ("UP" will now read backwards), and place template over the "flower" aligning the outline drawn on template. Mark fabric for cutting.

4. Cut, allowing for seam allowances.

A "paste up" is the only way to see exactly what your design will look like. Cut your designed pieces without seam allowances. Use glue stick on paper, and stick down the fabric pieces. Sometimes you will see that it would be better to align the "flower" differently. Sometimes you won't like it at all and will move on to some other design. Sometimes it looks even better than you thought it would!

Diamond (and parallelogram) designs using the reverse of the template are also interesting.

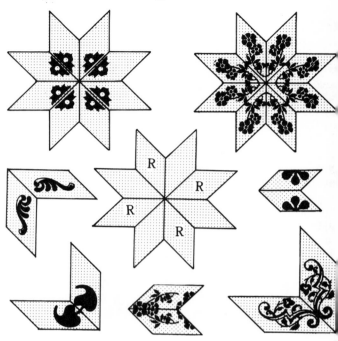

In these, every other template has been reversed

To do this reversal on the designed piece:

1. Turn fabric wrong-side up.

2. Place template (with "flower" design marked on it) over "flower." Template should be upside down ("UP" reading backwards). Mark for cutting.

3. Do not move fabric. Turn template over (so "UP" reads correctly) and move to another "flower." Align "flower" and mark for cutting.

4. Cut, allowing for seam allowances.

Perhaps you would like to alternate two printed designs.

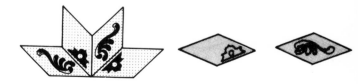

This doesn't require a reversal of templates, but it does require two templates. Each is marked with desired design.

The possibilities for using fabric prints are almost infinite and—like life—challenging, rewarding, disappointing, and full of surprises along the way.

Striped fabrics offer exciting design possibilities. This is illustrated in the "Las Doce" quilt on the inside back cover. This entire quilt was developed from a single large-striped fabric combined with a simple, plain tan all-over print. The same basic eight-pointed star pattern was used for all the blocks.

There are three kinds of stripes.

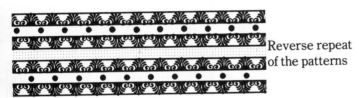

Repeat of a single stripe

Overall Stripes

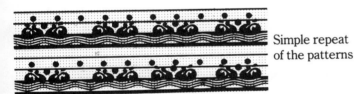

Reverse repeat of the patterns

Symmetrical Stripe

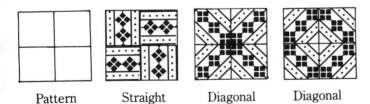

Simple repeat of the patterns

Asymmetrical (non-symmetric) Stripe

Any of the three types of stripes may be used in the following illustrations. It is very important that any intersections of stripes meet perfectly.

Striped fabric

Pattern   Straight   Diagonal   Diagonal

Larger striped prints offer a real bonanza for the six-inch block. The prints within the stripe can be used for small pieces without ever indicating at all that they are part of a stripe. Thus it is possible to get several coordinated prints and a stripe out of one larger striped fabric. This is how the fabric was used in "Las Doce" Quilt. Remember that more designing and use of a fabric requires more yardage.

 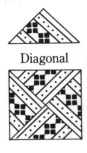 

Straight   Diagonal   Straight

1. With the fabric right-side up, place plastic template over stripes on fabric. Locate stripe exactly where you want it to appear. With permanent pen, draw on the plastic the simple outline of one (or more) of the stripes.

2. Write "UP" on the face of template on which you have drawn stripe.

3. Turn fabric wrong-side up. Turn template over ("UP" will now appear backwards), and place template over stripe aligning outline drawn on template. Mark fabric for cutting.

4. Cut, allowing for seam allowances.

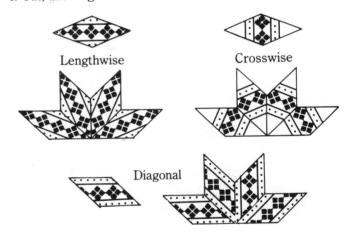

Lengthwise   Crosswise

Diagonal

Uses a simple repeat of the templates

Reverse alternate templates

If the design calls for every other template to be reversed, mark half of the pieces using template reading "UP" in step 3.

Use of Fabric—Stripes

As intriguing as stripes are, they do present some problems. For example:

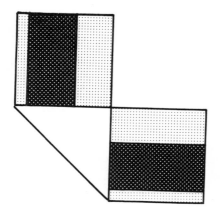

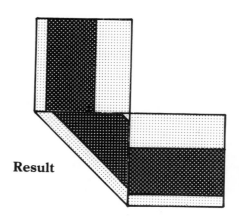

Result

In the triangle above, you would like to use the stripe so that the black stripe appears continuous. **This is mathematically impossible!** (This fact was such a comfort to me. I kept feeling I just wasn't doing something right.)

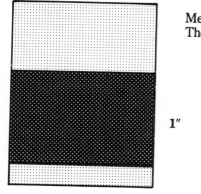

1″

Measure it—prove it to yourself.
The width in the triangular piece is almost 1½ times wider!

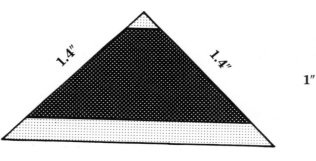

1.4″   1.4″

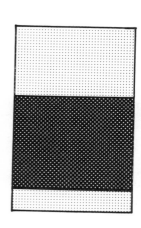

1″

A better solution may be to move the black stripe in the design:

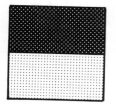

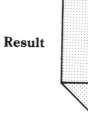

Result

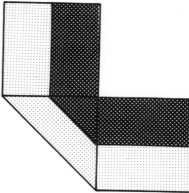

To do this, mark on the triangle template exactly where the edge of the black stripe meets the edge of the stripe on the other templates.

10

Setting the Blocks

Setting the Blocks

Careful consideration should be given to placement of blocks in the quilt. Blocks should be set so the designs, colors, light and dark contrast, and scale of the size of pieces in the blocks are all balanced and serve to enhance the appearance of the total quilt. To begin, pin the finished blocks to the wall and stand back. The best perspective for design is looking at something vertically. You cannot get the same perspective by laying your blocks out on a table or the floor. I cannot emphasize this strongly enough. **Pin them to the wall!**

Squint. See those lights? Balance them. Try one in the middle? One in each corner? All around the outside of the quilt? All the blocks circling the center block? Going diagonally across the quilt (in both directions)? Going horizontally and vertically across the quilt? All of these are possibilities for balancing the blocks.

Does one color or a strong "dark" or a "zinger" appear in only a few blocks? Balance them.

Is one pattern design different from the rest (circular, strong "X", strong "cross", strong star points, multitude of tiny pieces)? Feature it in your balance of the blocks.

Some of the blocks may contain several or all of the balancing problems. It is not easy. Work out the balance that seems best, leave it for a while, come back and see if you still like it. Ask opinions of others. Sometimes non-quiltmakers, especially children, give a fresh viewpoint to this balancing that we might have overlooked. Remember that you have the final say, so sew it together like you want it.

Since none of us is perfect, you sometimes find you have made a block that just doesn't fit in. Put it aside, and make another one that fits the need for balance in the quilt.

When a pleasing arrangement of blocks has been found, make a sketch outline of which blocks go where. It is also helpful to pin a label to each block. This label should give the location (Row 2 Block 3, for example) of the block in the quilt.

Row 1 Block 1	Row 2 Block 1	Row 3 Block 1
Row 1 Block 2	Row 2 Block 2	Row 3 Block 2
Row 1 Block 3	Row 2 Block 3	Row 3 Block 3
Row 1 Block 4	Row 2 Block 4	Row 3 Block 4

Master Square

Using the outside outline of any of the 6″ grids, make a template exactly 6″ square. See-through template material is preferred. Mark center points on each side and draw vertical and horizontal lines connecting these points. Draw diagonal lines from opposite corners. This is known as the "Master six-inch Square" and should be labelled as such.

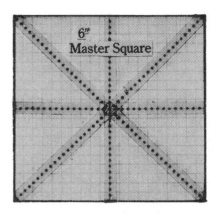

Trim any excess seam allowance on each block **except** for seam allowance on outside of the block. Place blocks wrongside up. Lay the Master Square on one block using the drawn lines to help center and align the template with the block. Using a different colored pencil than the one used to mark the sewing lines on the pieces, draw carefully around the Master Square. This will give you new sewing lines to sew the blocks together; it insures that each pieced block you sew to another is exactly square and the same size as every other block. Mark all the blocks in this manner.

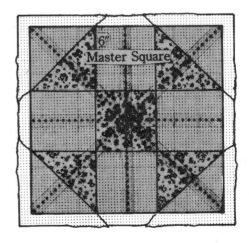

In aligning the Master Square on the block, do not mark off any of the sewn points. Sometimes some adjustments must be made or points altered so that this does not happen. Make a **very small** adjustment to the last ½″ of an outside seam on one side, and then do the same thing to the matching seam on the opposite side of the block. If necessary, adjust or alter the matching seams on the other two sides of the block.

Counterpane Set of the Blocks

Straight Set

Diagonal Set

Counterpane

A sampler quilt differs from a regular block-design quilt in that all (or many) of the blocks are different designs. Thus the blocks need to be set apart to make sure the different block designs are distinct. One way to do this is to use an unpieced, plain block between the pieced blocks. Every other block will be a pieced block. The plain blocks feature quilting. This method of setting blocks together is called "counterpane."

Balance of design in the total quilt is very important. The counterpane setting will be balanced if all four corners of the quilt have the same kind of block. All four must be pieced blocks; or all four must be counterpane blocks.

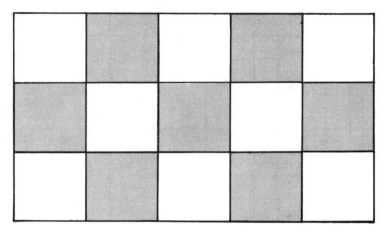

8 pieced blocks
7 counterpane blocks

Counterpane blocks must be marked with the Master Square on the wrong side of the fabric. Use the same color pencil that you used to mark the Master Square on pieced blocks. The quilting design may be marked on the plain counterpane blocks now or after the blocks are sewed together.

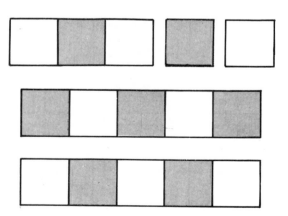

This is a straight set of the blocks. Setting sampler blocks together without counterpane or sashing is not recommended. Pin and sew blocks using the sewing lines marked from the Master Square. Sew the blocks together in rows. Then sew rows together.

9 pieced blocks   **8 triangles (half blocks)**
4 counterpane blocks   **4 corner triangles**

Each quilt block is the same size.

Side triangles are ½ the size of the block

Corner triangles are ¼ the size of the block

This gives the dimension for sewing. **Seam allowances must be added to the triangles.** Sew blocks and triangles together in rows. Then sew rows together.

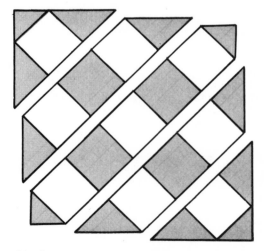

In setting blocks on the diagonal, the way the design of the block looks on the diagonal should be considered. A block set on the diagonal will give a different appearance than when set square. Sometimes it will be more pleasing; sometimes it is not good at all. If you intend to set the blocks on the diagonal, it is wise to look at each block on the diagonal before you piece it. If a pieced block doesn't work on the diagonal, set it aside and make another.

Sashing (or Stripping) the Blocks

Sashing

When the blocks are set apart by a strip of fabric, it is called sashing, stripping, or sometimes called lattice. Sashing frames each block and unifies the different blocks within its framework.

Fabric for sashing can be a solid or a print, but the first consideration should be that it enhances or "shows off" the blocks. Don't overlook the possibility of using a larger print stripe. Solid fabrics may have extra quilting designs. It is very important that all of the sashing be cut on the **straight grain of the fabric.**

Keep proportion in mind when planning your sashing. Sashing which is too wide will overwhelm the blocks, and too narrow a width seems weak. I consider maximum width of a border to be one third the width of a block. Less than that width usually looks better. With blocks set square, it works better visually if the vertical sashing is the longer (unseamed) and the horizontal is the shorter pieces. Cut your sashing pieces and label to make the right piece easy to find.

Square-Set Sashing

In straight-set blocks with sashing, sew the sashing between blocks to form rows. Then sew vertical sashing to rows, and join rows.

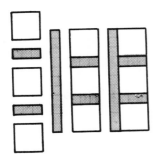

Sew outside sashing. Borders may be added.

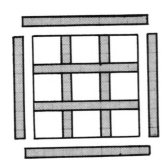

This outside sashing may be wider than the inside sashing, but it should never be narrower than the inside sashing. The wider outside sashing may be the border.

Diagonal-Set Sashing

In diagonal-set blocks with sashing, sew sashing between blocks and triangles to form rows. Sew vertical sashing to rows, and join rows.

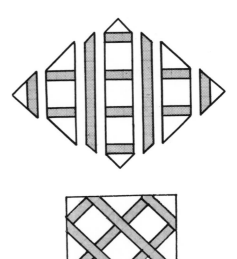

Sew outside sashing. Borders may be added.

This outside sashing may be wider than the inside sashing, but it should never be narrower than the inside sashing. The wider outside sashing may be the border.

Diagonal Set of the Blocks

Diagonal Set "A"

In diagonal set with sashing, there are different ways or points by which the sashing joins the border. This makes the triangular or "half blocks" a different size. Please see the following diagrams.

Diagonal Set "B"

Diagonal-Set Sashing

Diagonal-Set Sashing

Each quilt block is the same size.

Each triangle on every side is ½ the size of the quilt block.

The triangles at the four corners are ¼ the size of the quilt block.

All the blocks are the same size.

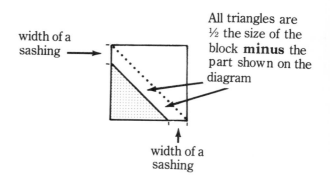

width of a sashing

All triangles are ½ the size of the block **minus** the part shown on the diagram

width of a sashing

This gives the dimension for sewing. **Seam allowances must be added to all triangles.**

This gives the dimension for sewing. **Seam allowances must be added to all triangles.**

Corners of the sashing are cut off by the border. It is best if the border here is different from the sashing.

Corners of blocks come to the edge of the borders. It is best if the border is different from the sashing.

Diagonal Set "C"

Diagonal-Set Sashing

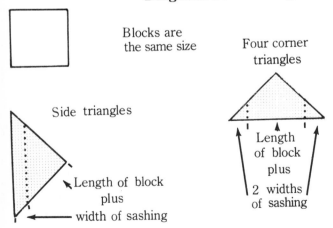

Blocks are the same size

Side triangles

Length of block plus width of sashing

Four corner triangles

Length of block plus 2 widths of sashing

This gives the dimension for sewing. **Seam allowances must be added to all triangles.**

The border may be different or the same as the sashing.

Latticework Sashing

Lattice

Each block is framed with narrow strips of the same color fabric. These framed blocks are then sashed with a narrow strip of another color. Strips of the framing fabric are then appliqued in an "X" across the intersections of the sashing. A good illustration of this type of lattice is Carol Goin's quilt "Turn About" on the inside back cover.

Intersection Squares

"Posts" or intersection squares may be used but should not be outstanding or highlights. In a sampler quilt the blocks should be the feature attraction.

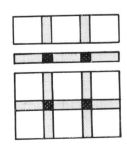

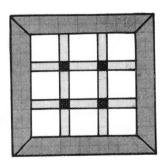

Borders

Borders

Borders are a very important part of the design of the sampler quilt. Without a border the quilt will seem incomplete. Borders may be simple or intricate, but they should incorporate elements of the quilt such as color, print of fabric, design and proportion.

Measurements for borders should be taken across the center of the quilt from edge to edge. This eliminates some of the stretch you tend to get when you measure along the outside edge of the quilt. Be sure to include the width of two borders when cutting each of the border pieces. A safety factor of an extra 4″ will allow you to miter corners. (This total of 4″ comes from a 2″ safety factor at each end of the border.)

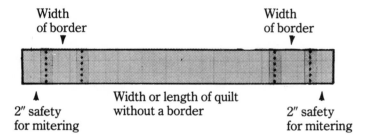

Width of border ▼   Width of border ▼

▲ 2″ safety for mitering   Width or length of quilt without a border   ▲ 2″ safety for mitering

Mark the center point of each side of the unbordered quilt. Mark the center point of each border piece. (Simply fold it in half and mark with a pin.) Pin center points of border pieces to center points of the quilt. Carefully pin from these center points to each edge. Sew the border to the quilt. Sew top and bottom borders first, then sew the two side borders.

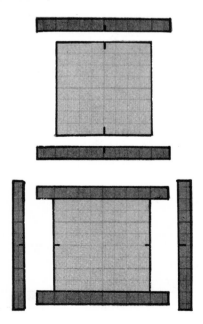

When multiple borders are desired, sew the multiple borders together. Then fit and join the whole border unit to the quilt. **Caution.** You must include the two widths of the "total multiple border" plus the 4″ miter safety allowance when measuring for border lengths.

In diagonal setting, triangles on the edges and corners may be used as a design part of the borders. This can be done by choosing color, fabric or design for them. Triangles with stripes along the outer edge are seen as an actual part of the border. This was done in "Los Trece" quilt on the inside front cover of the book.

A border of one of the darker colors in the quilt usually works best along the outside of the quilt. It helps define and identify the outer limit of the quilt. With a light outside border, the quilt just seems to drift off, and there is no definite stopping place or "fence."

A large print or stripe with a print in it can often be used to advantage in a border. The prints should be cut so the same part of the print appears at the corners. To do this takes planning before you cut.

Put 2 pins through two exact center points of two identical flowers (or other prominent outlines in the print). Fold the fabric so the 2 pins fall exactly on top of each other. Mark this center fold.

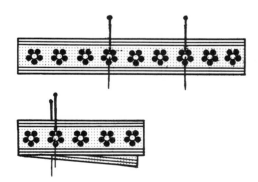

Pin this center fold point to the center of your unbordered quilt. Then the corners should have the same part of the print of the fabric. (The "flower" you pinned through will not necessarily be at the corners.)

Drafting Narrow Borders

One of the light, bright or "zinger" colors makes a real highlight when used as a narrow inner border. A very narrow border is even more dramatic. It will really stand out, so it must be straight. The **very** narrow (less than ½") borders should be more precisely pieced by hand. For example:

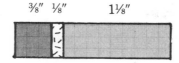

3⁄8"   1⁄8"   1 1⁄8"

This border series is planned for the quilt.

Mark fabrics this way:

Border No. 1

¼" — Seam allowance

— Cutting line

— Sewing line A

3⁄8" — Border

— Sewing line B

¼" — Seam allowance

······ Future cutting line

1" — Handle

— Cutting line

Border No. 2

¼" — Seam allowance — Cutting line

— Sewing line A

1⁄8" — Border — Sewing line B

¼" — Seam allowance

······ Future cutting line

1" — Handle

— Cutting line

Border No. 3

¼" — Seam allowance — Cutting line

— Sewing line A

1 1⁄8" — Border

— Sewing line B

¼" — Seam allowance

······ Future cutting line

1" — Handle

— Cutting line

Unless the fabric is cut with the "handle," the narrow strip will twist and stretch out of shape. This extra "handle" allows you to have enough fabric to hold and sew.

Pin border #1 to border #2 exactly on sewing lines A. Sew, checking to see that all stitches are exactly on both sewing lines. Trim the "handle" off of border #2. Press seam allowances **away** from border #2.

Pin sewing line B of border #2 to sewing line A of border #3. Sew, checking to see that all stitches are exactly on both sewing lines. Press the seam allowance **toward** border #2. Cut the "handle" off border #1 and border #3.

Mitering the corners gives a very planned, concise finish to the borders. All stripes and multiple borders should have perfect intersections at the corners.

Use of the Grid

In 1979 Jinny Beyer published her book *Patchwork Patterns* in which she developed and explained the use of a "grid system" for accurate drafting of geometric patterns. I believe this to be the best system for drafting accurate designs and the most stable system to classify quilt block patterns. Therefore, I have incorporated the grid system for drafting such patterns and for organizing the patterns into groups or "patch families."

The basis for the "grid system" is to divide the desired block size into equal sections. This is done by dividing each side of block into equal divisions and then drawing straight lines between division points on parallel sides of the block. This makes a "grid" for the block.

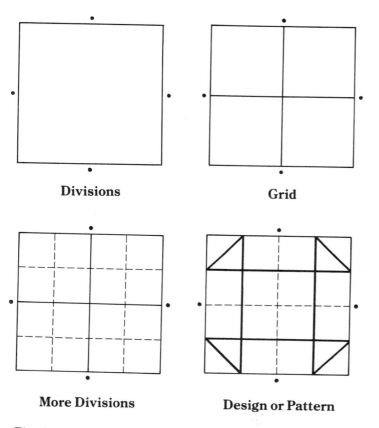

Divisions   **Grid**

More Divisions   **Design or Pattern**

The design or pattern is created using the lines and points of intersection of the lines of the grid. By placing a piece of tracing paper over a grid, different designs may be made using the same grid.

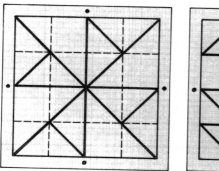

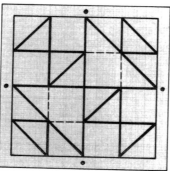

Designs on Tracing Paper

Four-Patch Pattern

Each side of desired size quilt block is divided into 2 equal divisions, then 4 equal divisions, then 8 equal divisions.

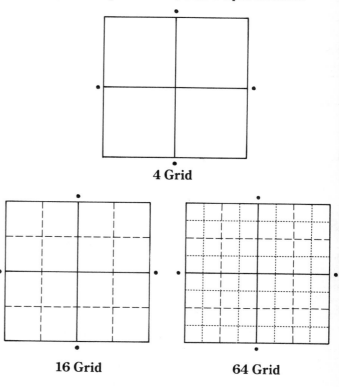

4 Grid

16 Grid   **64 Grid**

Nine-Patch Pattern

Each side of desired size quilt block is divided into 3 equal divisions, then 6 equal divisions, then 12 equal divisions.

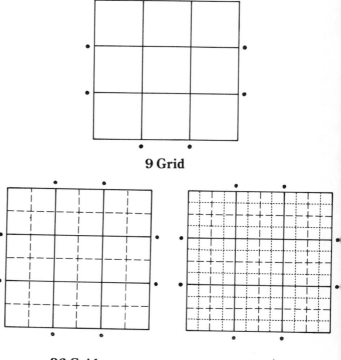

9 Grid

36 Grid   **144 Grid**

18

Five-Patch Pattern

Each side of desired size quilt block is divided into 5 equal divisions, then 10 equal divisions.

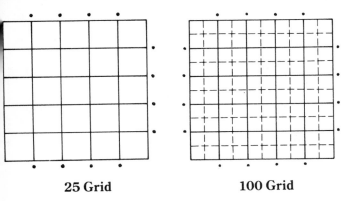

25 Grid   **100 Grid**

Seven-Patch Pattern

Each side of desired size quilt block is divided into 7 equal divisions. Seven-Patch patterns are seldom divided into more than the 49 grid.

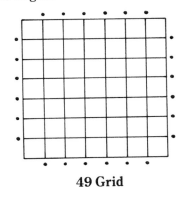

49 Grid

Eight-Pointed Star Pattern

Each side of desired size block is divided into 2 equal sections of a "unit size," and 1 middle section of "unit size" multiplied by 1.41. (1.41 is the square root of 2. Mathematicians will probably cringe at the following, but we less mathematics-inclined quilters may think of 1.41 as one of several "magic numbers." We don't need to know their derivation, simply that they work.)

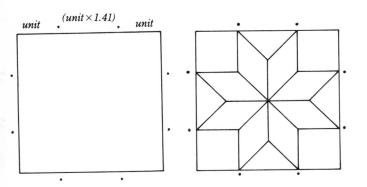

In an Eight-Pointed Star pattern there are only two dimensions other than the size of the block. All "a" dimensions are the same and equal. Also, all "b" dimensions are the same and equal.

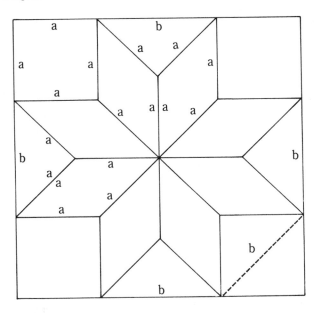

Dimension "a" may be found by dividing the size of the block by 3.41. (3.41 is the sum of all dimensions around the side; another "magic number".)

   a = size of side of block divided by 3.41

   b = a multiplied by 1.41.

For example:

   With a six-inch block

      a = 6 ÷ 3.41 or 1.76″ (Use 1¾″)

      b = 1.76 × 1.41 or 2.48 (Use 2½″)

All diamond shapes in an Eight-Pointed Star are 45° diamonds. (360° divided by 8 = 45°)

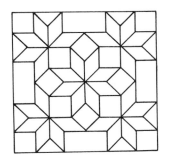 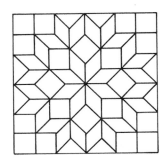

More intricate Eight-Pointed Star patterns may have divisions and dimensions which are multiples of the "unit a" and "unit × 1.41" (which is "Unit b.")

An easy way to handle the decimal values is to use a ruler divided into "10ths."

Curved-Line Pattern

Any square block pattern with a curved line falls in this category. The pattern may use any grid or may be based on the parts of a circle.

Four-Patch Pattern Grid

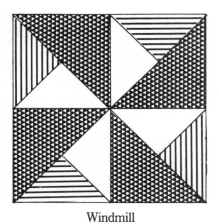

Windmill

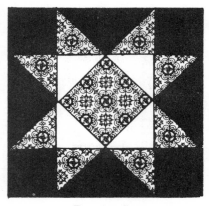

Evening Star

Old Tippecanoe

16-Grid   6″ Block

Four-Patch Pattern

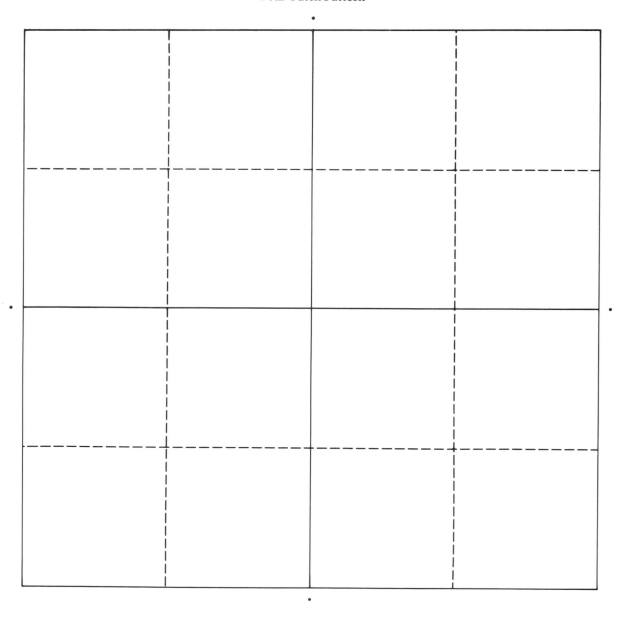

Four-Patch Pattern Grid

Jack-in-the-Pulpit

Kansas Troubles

Crow's Foot

64-Grid **6″ Block**

Four-Patch Pattern

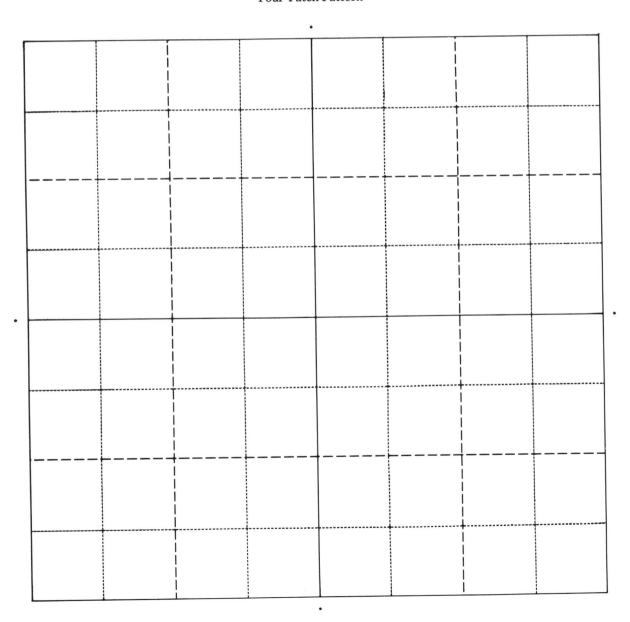

Old Maid's Ramble

Four-Patch Pattern

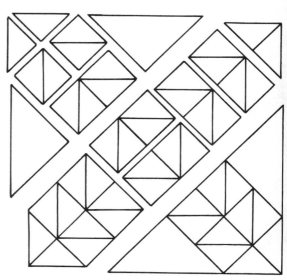

6″
Block

Piecing Assembly

Complex-looking pattern of simple construction. All pieces are triangles. Sew together to form three sections which are then sewn together.

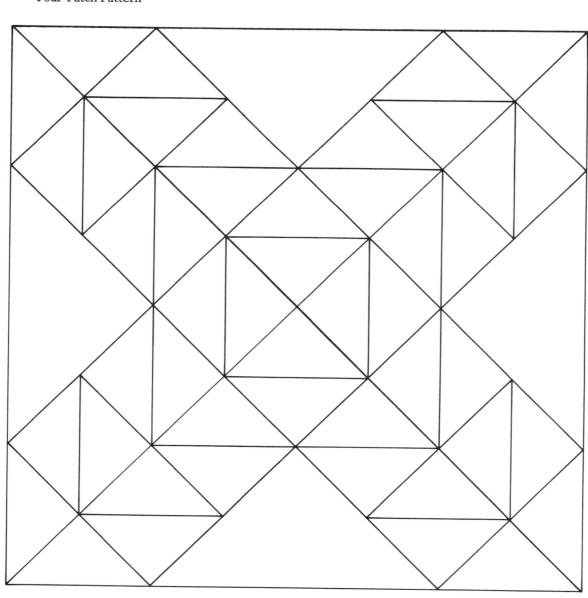

22

Devil's Claws

6″
Block

Four-Patch Pattern

Piecing Assembly

Outside pieces should be cut on the straight grain of the fabric if possible. Use of fabrics can make this seem like a "leaf" or "lily" design.

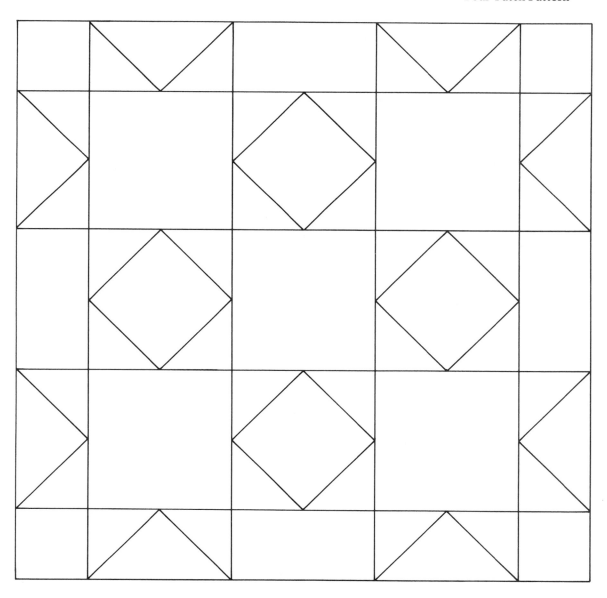

Blackford's Beauty

Four-Patch Pattern

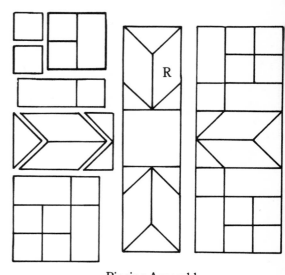

6"
Block

Piecing Assembly

Reverse R template. When sewing, check that each outside cor-
ner square is of the same fabric. Traditionally a dark fabric is
featured somewhere in the design.

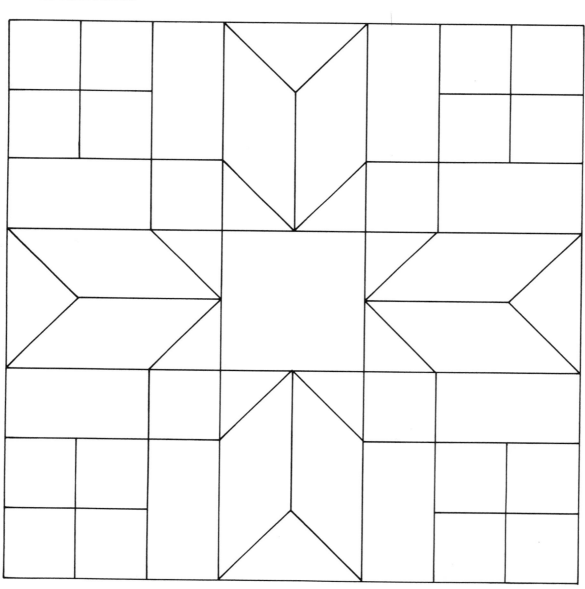

Star of Many Points

Piecing Assembly

6"
Block

Four-Patch Pattern

Reverse R Template. A "cross" or an "arrows" design depends upon which adjacent parallelograms are of same fabric. Same fabric on every other parallelogram gives "folded" effect.

R

Odd Fellow's Chain

Four-Patch Pattern

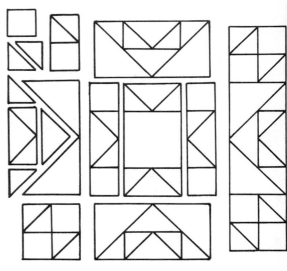

6″
Block

Piecing Assembly

Sew pieces into sections; sew sections into three rows; sew rows together. Use of variations of light and dark colored fabric enhance the design of this block.

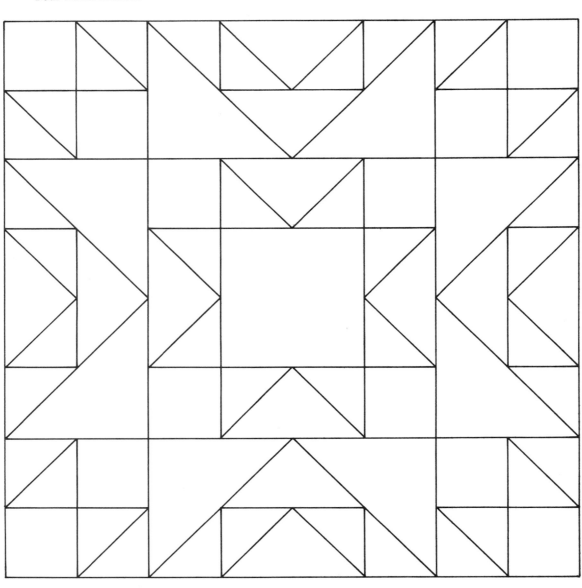

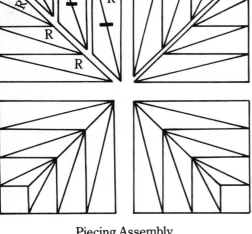

6"
Block

Piecing Assembly

Four-Patch Pattern

Reverse R *templates. Marking triangle templates and fabrics with a "joining mark" aids sewing the correct sides of the triangles together. Turn center points for variation.*

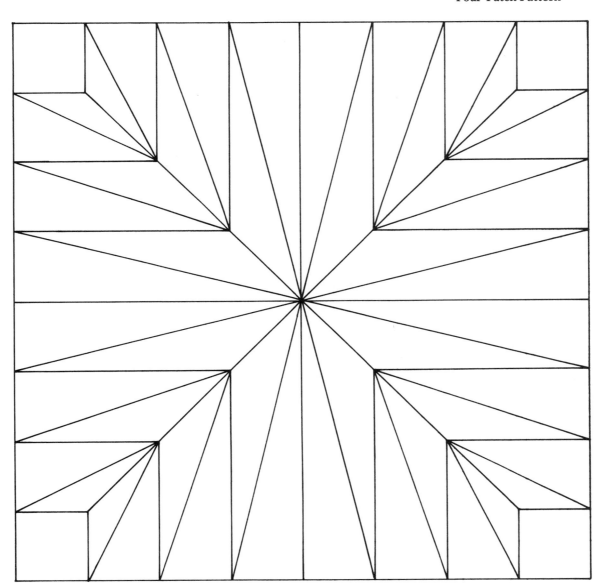

Nine-Patch Pattern Grid

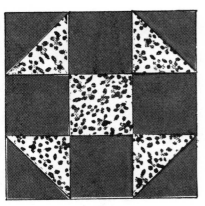

Shoo Fly

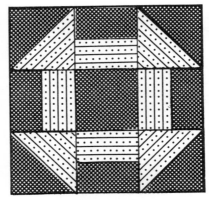

Monkey Wrench

54-40 or Fight

36-Grid   6″ Block

Nine-Patch Pattern

Night and Noon

Swing in the Center

Golgotha

144-Grid   **6″ Block**

Nine-Patch Pattern

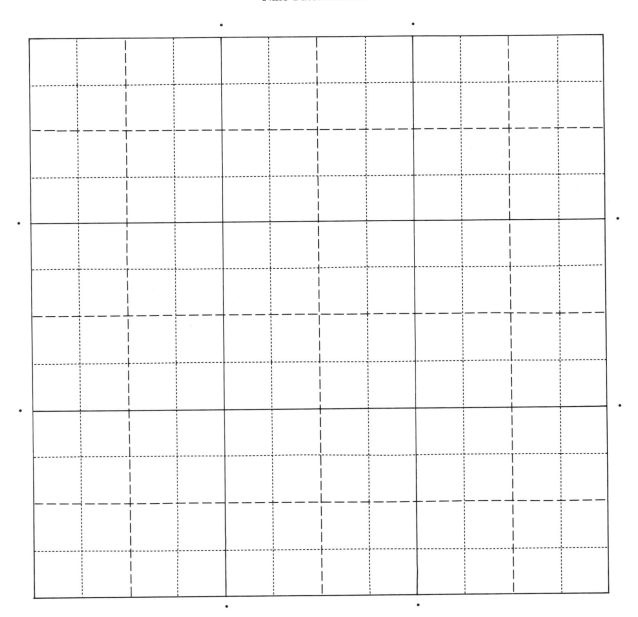

Rolling Stone

Nine-Patch Pattern

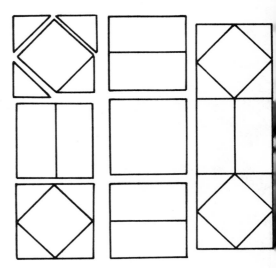

6″
Block

Piecing Assembly

Mathematically impossible to make a stripe on the diagonal side of four center triangles perfectly match up with same stripe on the length of the adjoining rectangular pieces.

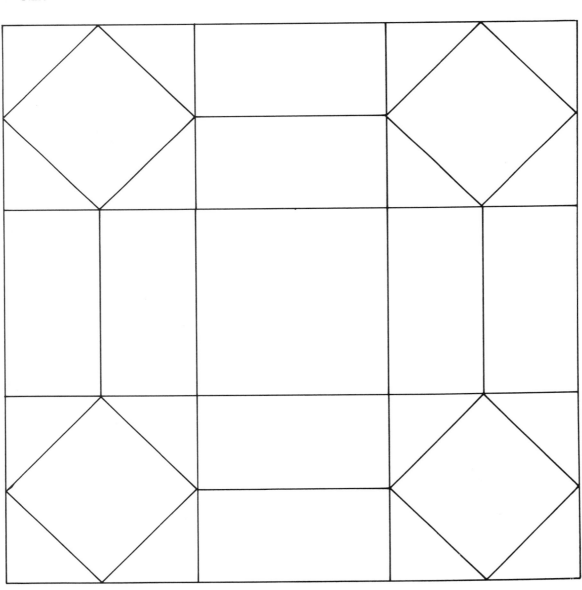

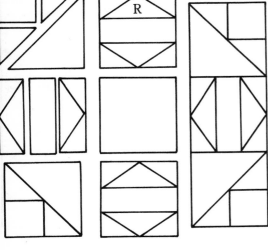

Piecing Assembly

Joseph's Coat

6"
Block

Nine-Patch Pattern

Elongated triangles make this block design seem to have a slight curve or bulge. This can be accented by using high contrast of light and dark colored fabrics.

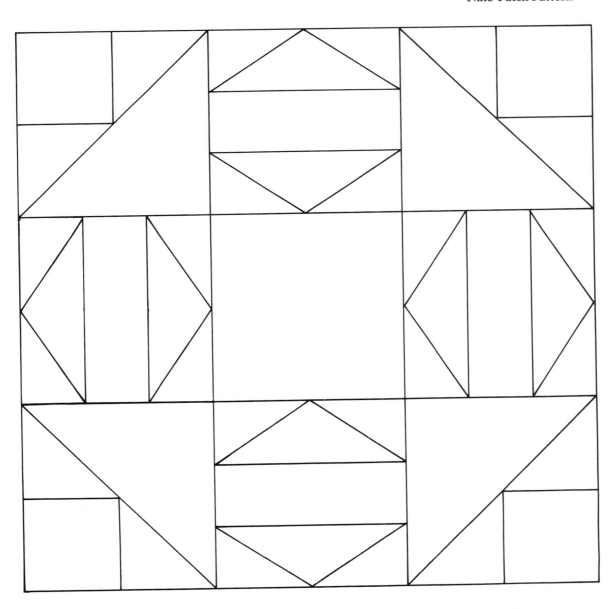

Arizona (Variation)

Nine-Patch Pattern

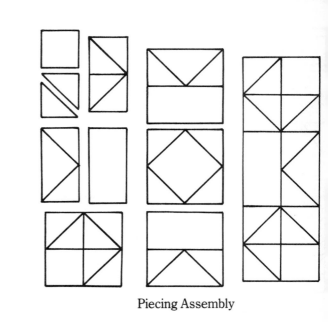

6″
Block

Piecing Assembly

Assembly is straightforward by rows. Experiment with fabric designs to make it seem intricate. If possible, place outside triangles and squares on straight grain of fabric.

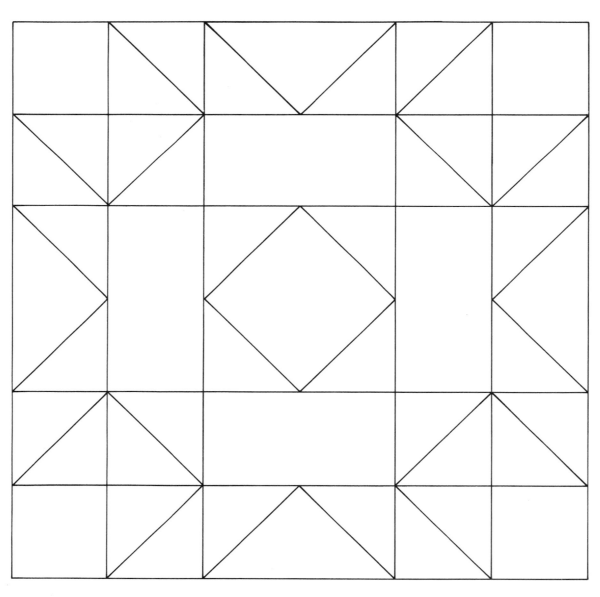

Mrs. Cleveland's Choice

6"
Block

Piecing Assembly

Best if long pieces are on straight grain of fabric. Center patch is almost a miniature of whole block. Block is good for either straight or diagonal set block.

Nine-Patch Pattern

Interlocked Square

Nine-Patch Pattern

6"
Block

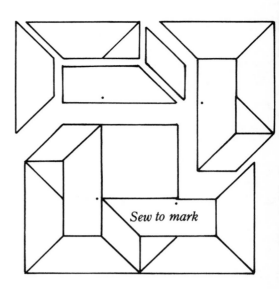

Piecing Assembly

Sew seams only from mark to mark. Knot off. Sew next seam mark to mark. Don't sew around corners. Suggest a fabric "past up" to assure right fabric placement. Try stripes.

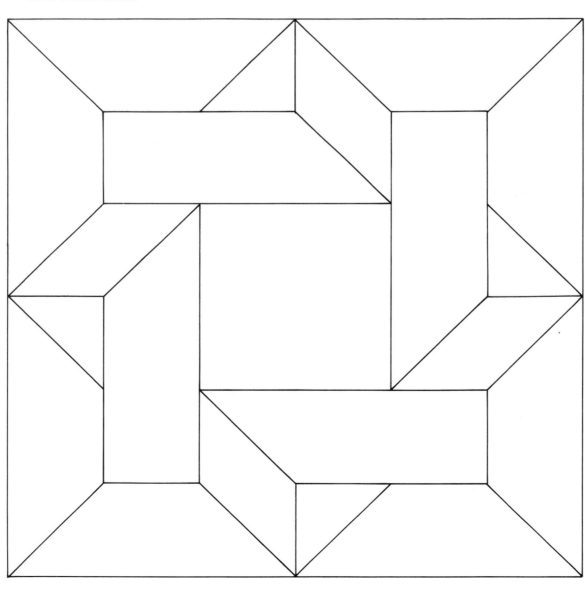

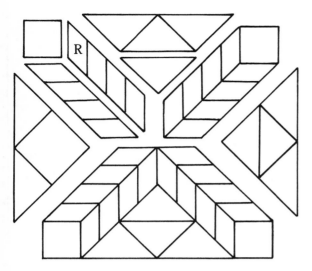

Piecing Assembly

Wood Lily

6"
Block

Reverse Ṙ template for matching adjacent piece. Sew these parallelogram pieces together in rows. Try "chevron" effect with stripes, or radiating effect with a color gradation.

Nine-Patch Pattern

35

Dolly Madison Star

Nine-Patch Pattern

6"
Block

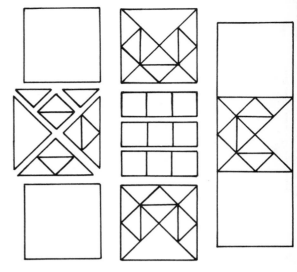

Piecing Assembly

Block designed on a mixed grid. The "nine-patch" in center square does not fit on same nine-patch grid as rest of the block. Center square is simply divided into a nine patch.

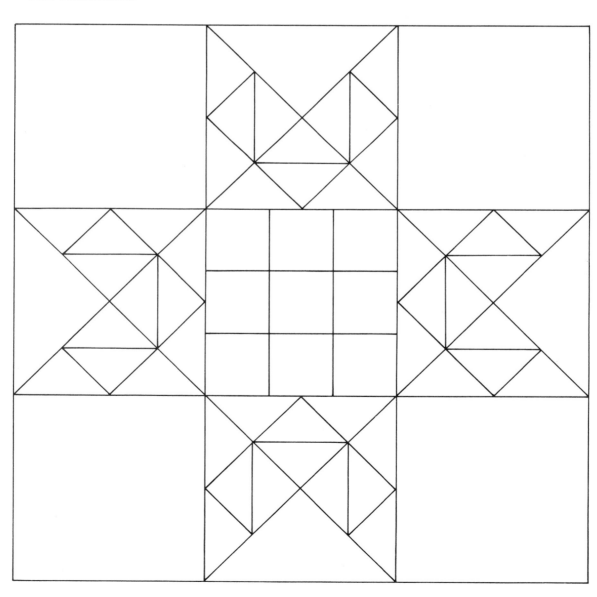

Rolling Echoes

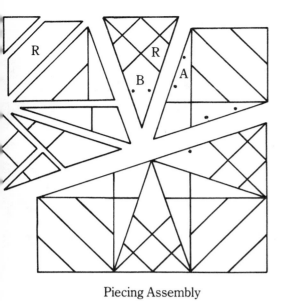

Piecing Assembly

6″
Block

Original Design
Catherine H. Anthony
1983

Nine-Patch Pattern

Reverse R templates. While sewing "pie-shaped" sections, it helps to mark a "joining mark" in the seam allowance of the two sections (A, B). Make in two major sections; join.

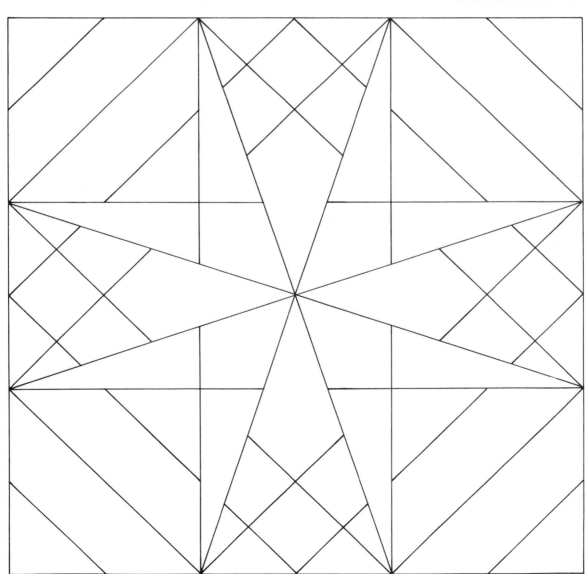

Five-Patch Pattern Grid

Jack in the Box

Providence

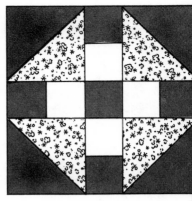

Double Wrench

100-Grid   **6″ Block**

Five-Patch Pattern

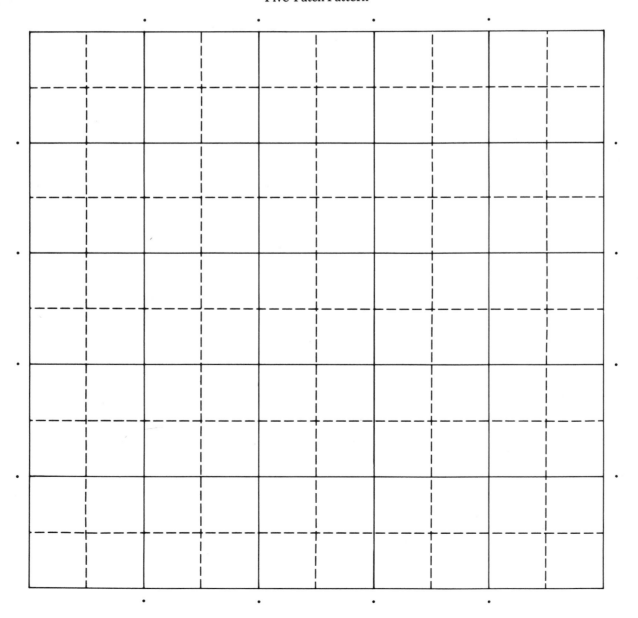

Cross and Crown

Piecing Assembly

6"
Block

Five-Patch Pattern

...her the cross in the center or the four crowns in the corners
...y be accented, depending on the way the fabric is used. Rela-
...ly larger pieces allow larger prints or striped fabric to be used
...dvantage.

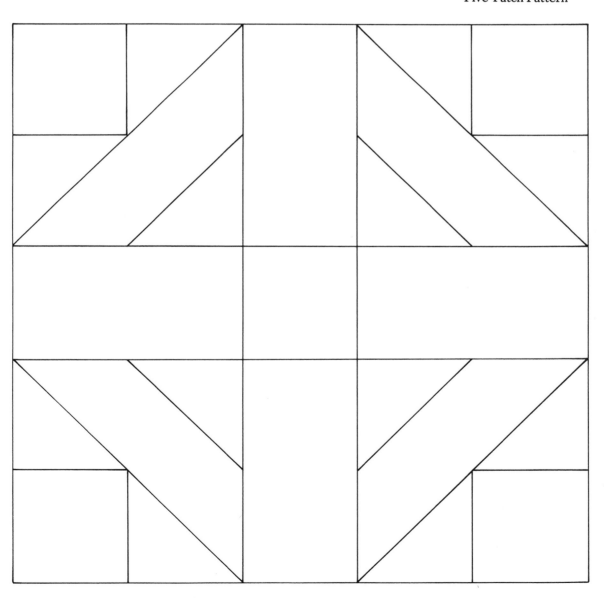

All Kinds

Five-Patch Pattern

6″
Block

Piecing Assembly

The four corner triangles must be the same fabric as block edge pieces (or a dark accent color) to keep the block from appearing as an unequal octagon instead of a square.

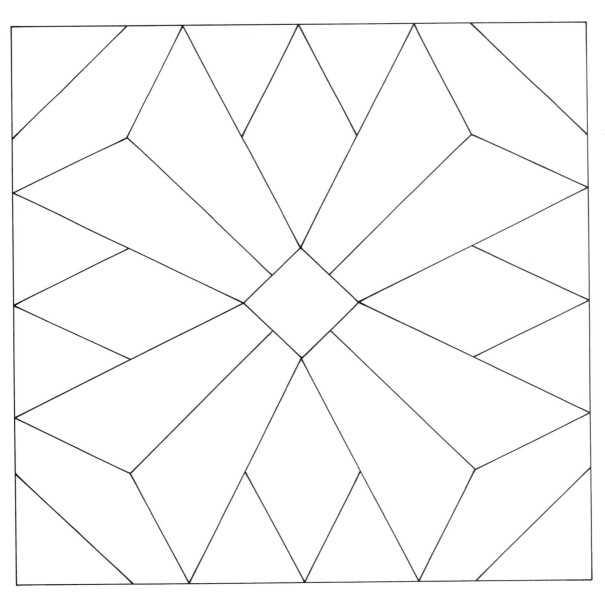

Japanese Poppy

6"
Block

Piecing Assembly

Five-Patch Pattern

Reverse R template. Make two corner sections, then middle diagonal row. Good as either a diagonal or straight-set block.

R

41

Seven-Patch Pattern Grid

Dove in the Window

Our Country

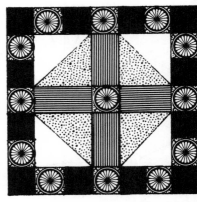

Lincoln's Platform

49-Grid   6″ Block

Seven-Patch Pattern

Hen and Chickens

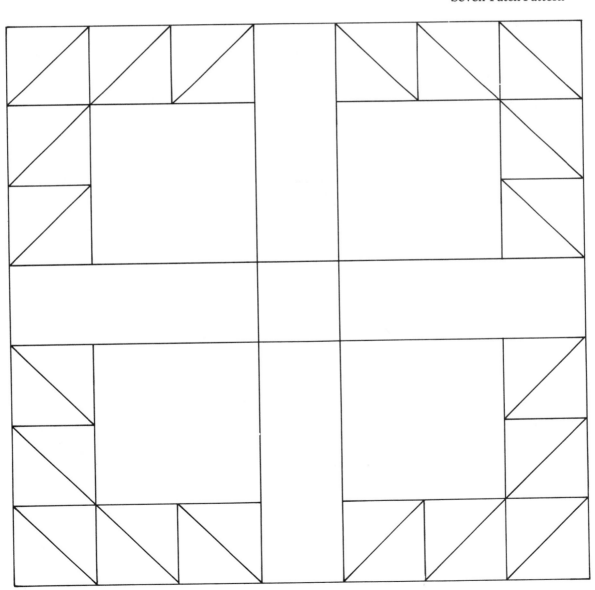

Piecing Assembly

Many smaller pieces around outside of block sometimes make finished block larger than desired. Check sewing lines on fabrics often to see that seam is on both marks exactly.

6″
Block

Seven-Patch Pattern

Prickly Pear

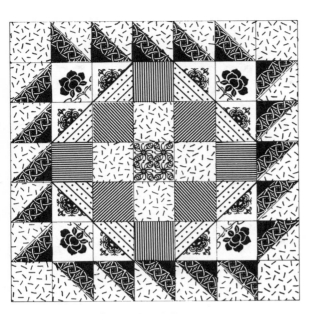

Seven-Patch Pattern

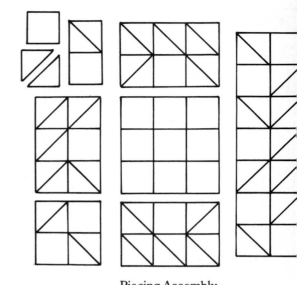

6"
Block

Piecing Assembly

Lots of pieces; only simple squares and triangles that fit together easily. But watch carefully the direction each of the color triangles points. That can be tricky.

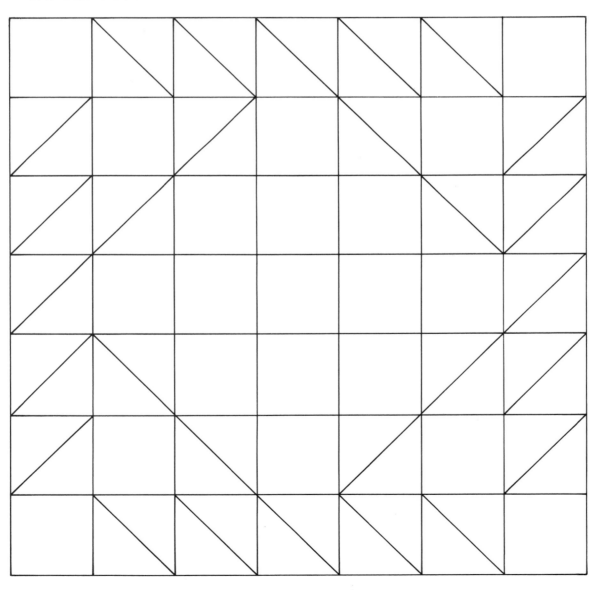

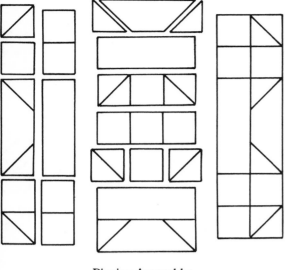

Piecing Assembly

Greek Cross

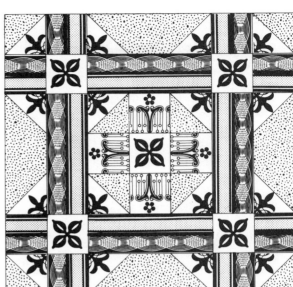

6"
Block

Seven-Patch Pattern

Important that the larger outside pieces have the straight grain of the fabric running parallel to the edge of block. This design can give an open grillwork effect.

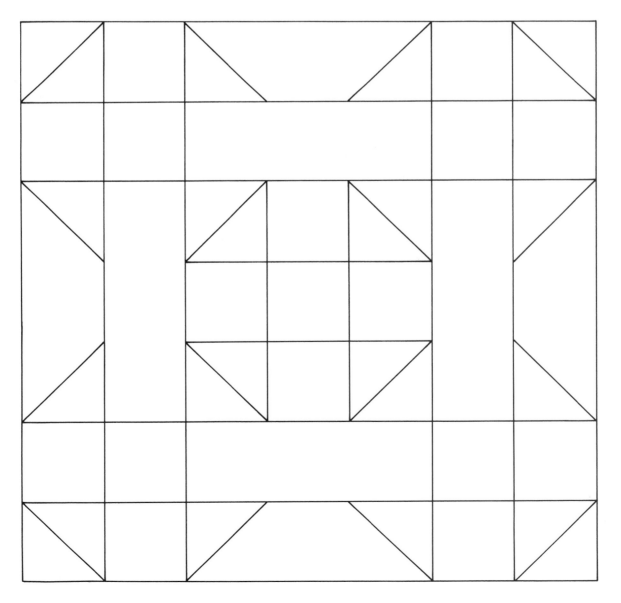

Bear's Paw

Seven-Patch Pattern

6″
Block

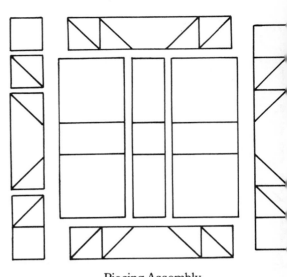

Piecing Assembly

Most variations of this pattern occur in the four larger squares. Each can be divided into triangles or four smaller squares. The center "cross" may be extended to block edge.

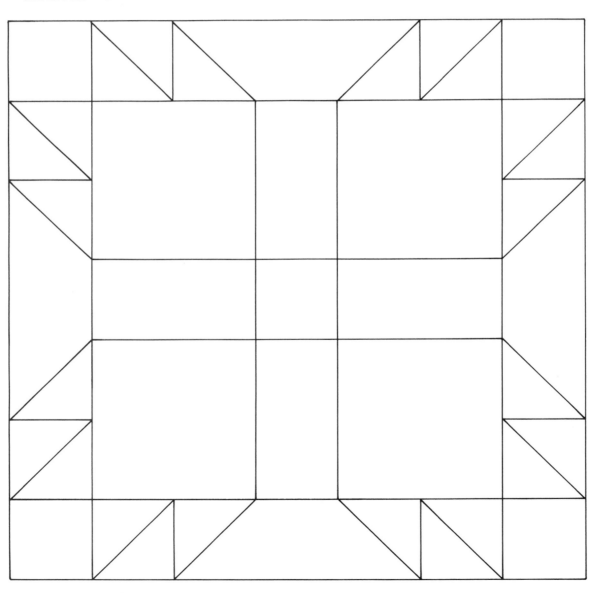

Twisted Ribbon

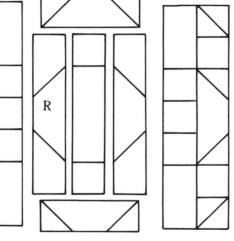

Piecing Assembly

6″
Block

Original Design
Janice Knapp
Quilters Newsletter
Feb. 1976

Reverse R template. Use utmost care that each fabric piece is in its proper position; otherwise design will be lost. A stripe fabric to twist and turn works best.

Seven-Patch Pattern

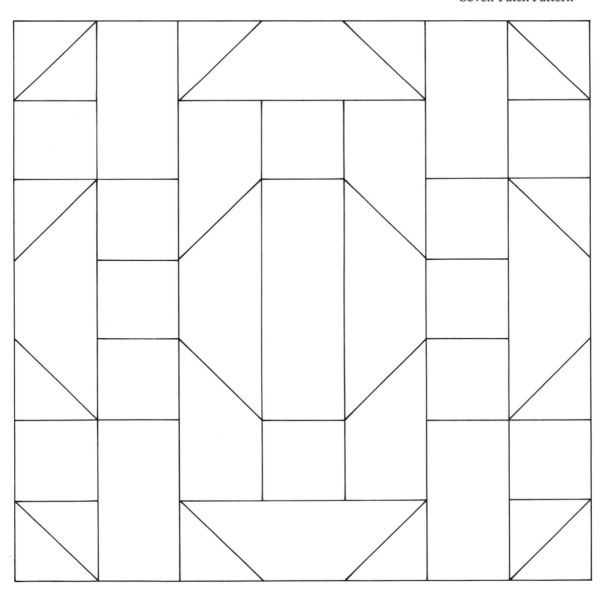

Eight-Pointed Star Patterns

LeMoyne Star

Silver and Gold

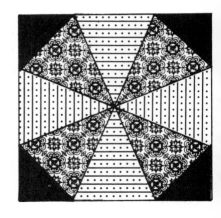

Kaleidoscope

Striped Star

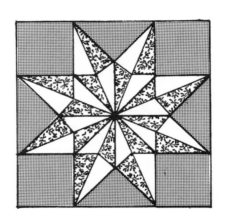

Saint Louis Star

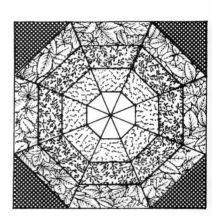

Spiderweb

Morning Star

Virginia Star

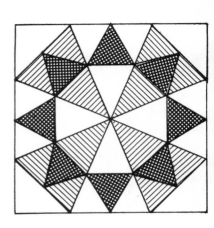

Evening Star

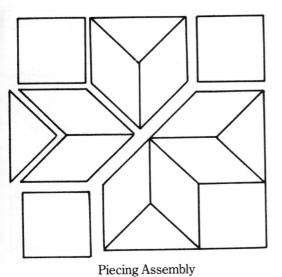

Piecing Assembly

Eight-Pointed Star Pattern Basic Grid

Eight-Pointed Star
Join two diamonds, attach the triangle. Make four of these units. Sew two diamond units together to make half of star. Attach one corner square to each half of star. Join the two halves of star. Attach last two corner units to star.

Eight-Pointed Star Basic Grid   6″ Block

Eight-Pointed Star Pattern

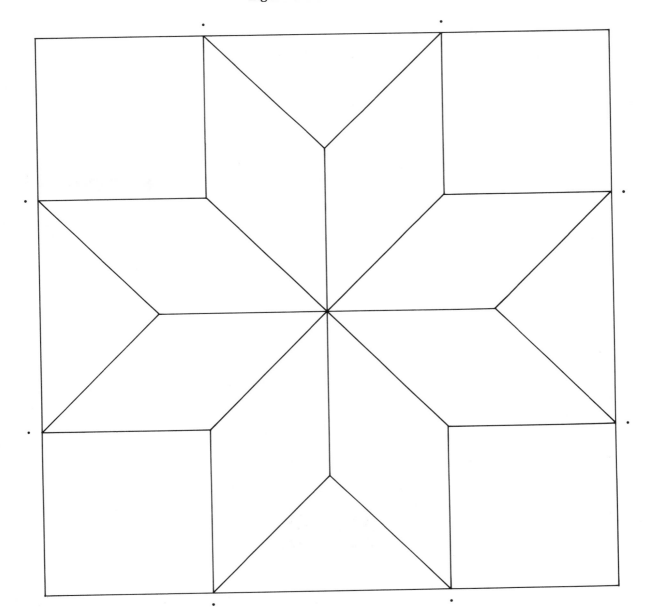

Blazing Star

Eight-Pointed Star Pattern

6"
Block

Piecing Assembly

Sew two diamonds in a row. Sew two rows to make a diamond. Make eight diamonds. Sew triangles to other pieces to make triangles and squares. Sew basic Eight-Pointed star order.

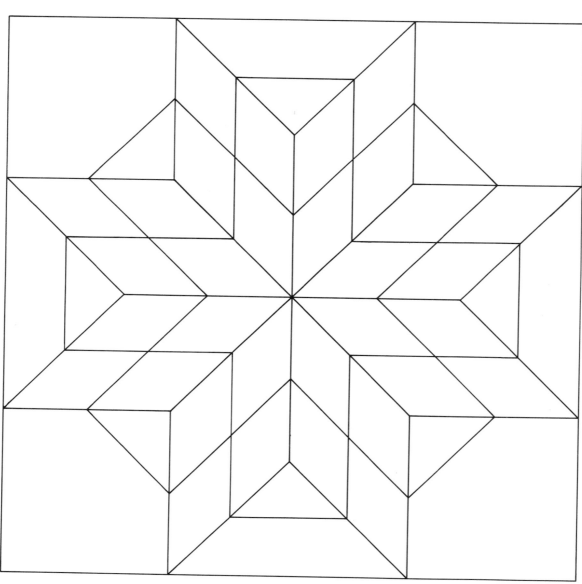

50

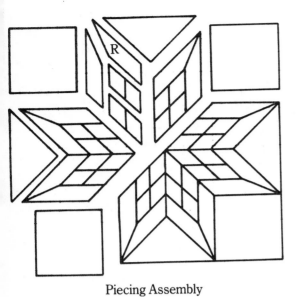

Piecing Assembly

Patty's Star

6"
Block

Eight-Pointed Star Pattern

Reverse R template. Sew two diamonds in a row. Sew two rows together. Then attach two long pieces to make diamond. Make eight diamonds. Sew in basic Eight-Pointed star sequence.

Swallows in Flight

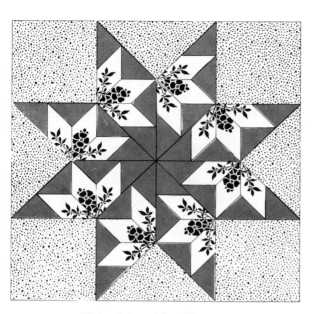

Eight-Pointed Star Pattern

6"
Block

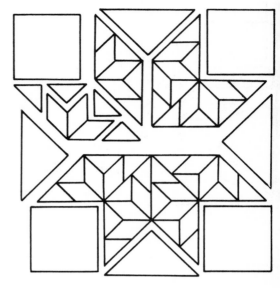

Piecing Assembly

Make a large diamond by joining three small diamonds; then attach four small triangles. Make eight such diamonds. Sew in basic Eight-Pointed Star sequence.

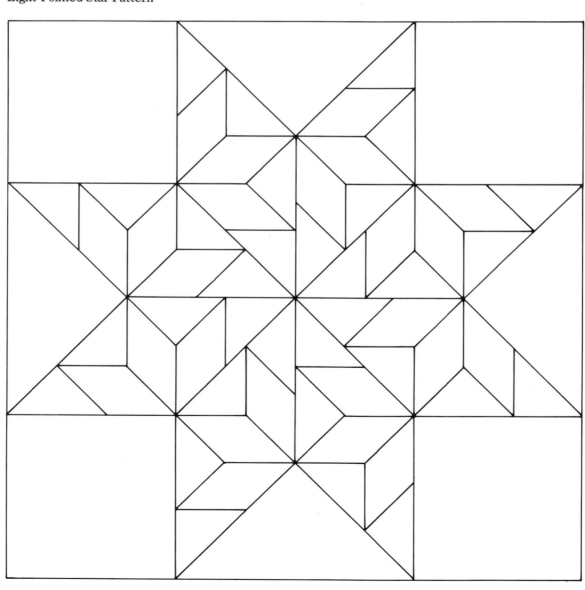

Radiant Star

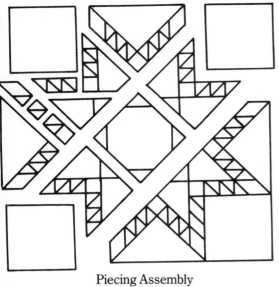

Piecing Assembly

6″
Block

Eight-Pointed Star Pattern

Make in three major sections; join, and then set in last two corner squares. The smallest triangles are joined on their longest sides to make squares. Patience. These are trying.

53

Castle Wall

Eight-Pointed Star Pattern

6″
Block

Piecing Assembly

Make two halves of octagon-shaped center and join to four center squares. Attach corner units. Attach four wedge-shapes in middle of each block. A very popular block.

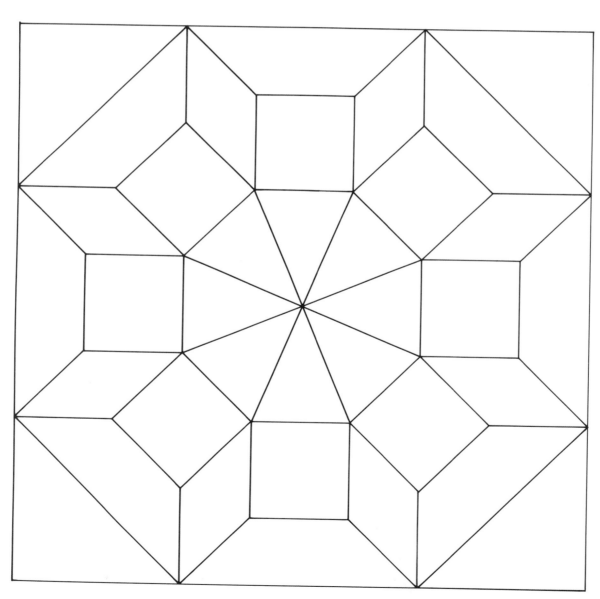

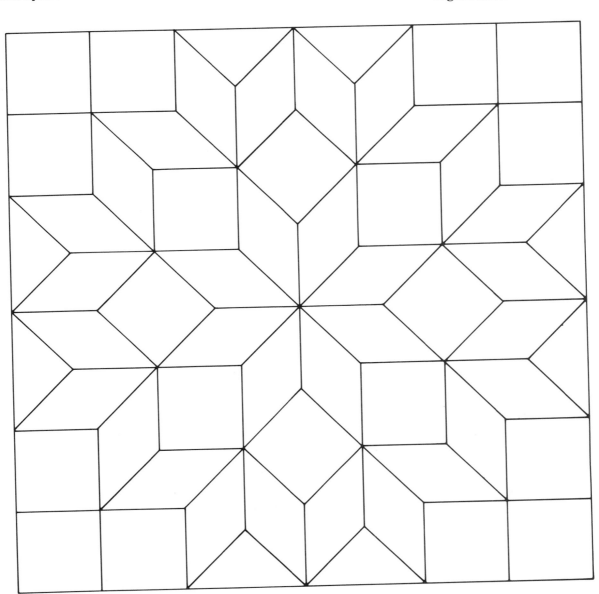

Carpenter's Wheel

6"
Block

Eight-Pointed Star Pattern

Intricate block uses only three templates, with R template reversed. Join two halves of the star in the middle. Fill in with the pieced units attached to squares "A".

Piecing Assembly

R

A

A

Curved-Line Patterns

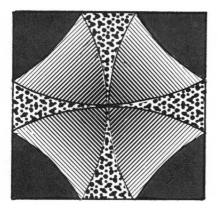

Winding Ways

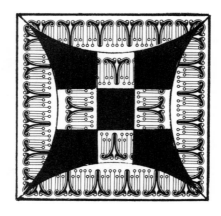

Glorified Nine Patch

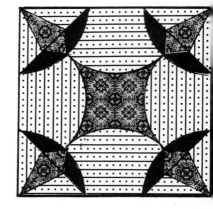

Turkey Tracks

Orange Peel

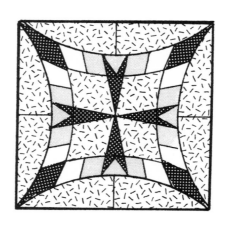

Chimney Swallows

Dusty Miller

Robbing Peter to Pay Paul

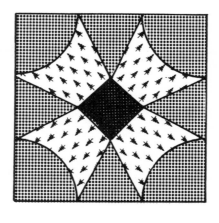

Greek Cross

French Star

56

Curved-Line Patterns

Curved-line patterns may be made on any of the block grids, the only difference from the regular block being that the pattern contains a curved line as part of the design. A curved-line pattern may also be designed from parts of a circle, and no grid is involved. Jinny Beyers, in *Patchwork Patterns,* gives excellent directions for drawing many of the more complex curved-line patterns.

Royal Cross
Nine-Patch Grid
Curved-Line Pattern

Strawberry
Designed from parts of a circle
Curved-Line Pattern

For drawing a simple curved line between two points on a design, any circular object of approximately the right diameter may be used (a paper cup, roll of masking tape, jar lid, plate, etc.).

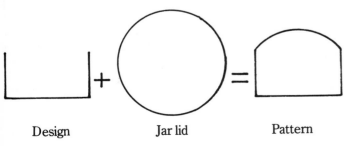

Design   Jar lid   Pattern

All curved-line templates should be marked with "joining marks." These "joining marks" are then marked in the seam allowance of the pattern.

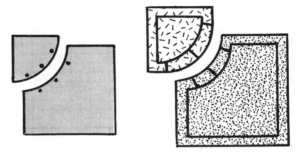

Curved seams in quilt making are sewed much the same as any other patchwork seam. The two pieces are pinned in place and then sewed. With curved seams it is easier if the curved out piece (like a ball) is placed under the curved over piece (like a baseball glove). End points and all "joining marks" of the two pieces are pinned through both sewing lines. Use more pins along the sewing lines until there is a pin every ½".

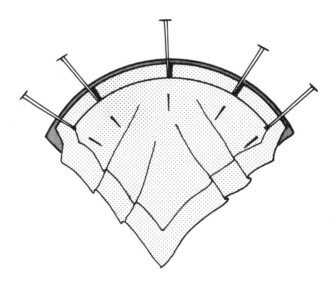

Sew, checking to see that all stitches are on both sewing lines. Remove pins as you come to them. Do not pull stitches too tight as this will put gathers along the seam. Do not clip; this weakens the seam.

Pressing the curved-seam pieces usually works best if you press the seam allowance of the curved-out (convex) piece towards the receiving (curved-in, or concave) piece.

Curved seam blocks should be pressed from the top of the block.

Royal Cross

Curved-Line Pattern

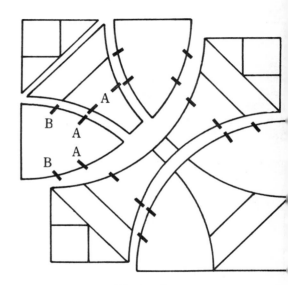

6"
Block

Piecing Assembly

Mark all curved pieces with "joining marks" (A,B). Curves are gentle and fit together simply. Make in three sections and join.

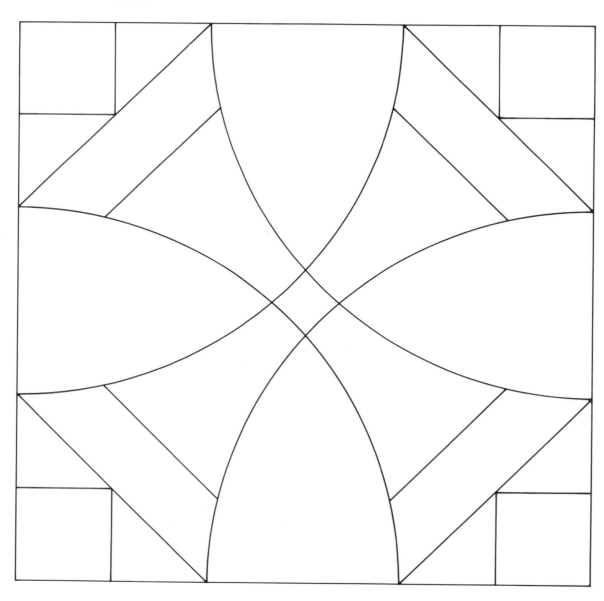

Twinkling Stars

6"
Block

Piecing Assembly

*Reverse R template. Mark curved pieces with "joining marks"
(A,B). Make diamonds. Sew two halves of the star; join. Sew
triangle wedges between star points. Sew curved corners.*

Curved-Line Pattern

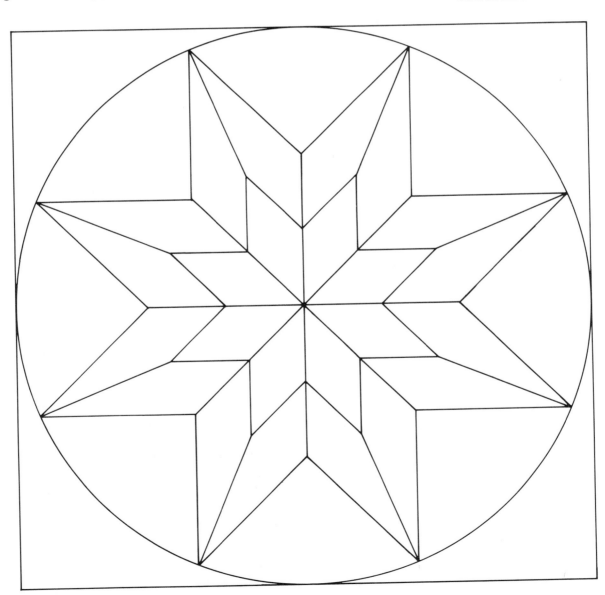

59

Hands All Around

Curved-Line Pattern

6"
Block

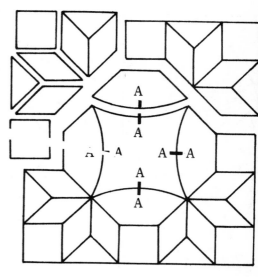

Piecing Assembly

Mark curved pieces with "joining marks" (A). Four curved pieces attach to the center curved piece. Four corner units with diamonds attach to whole central unit.

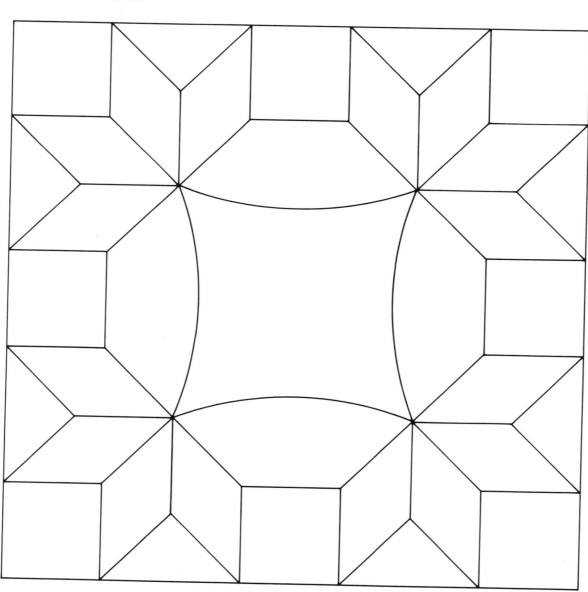

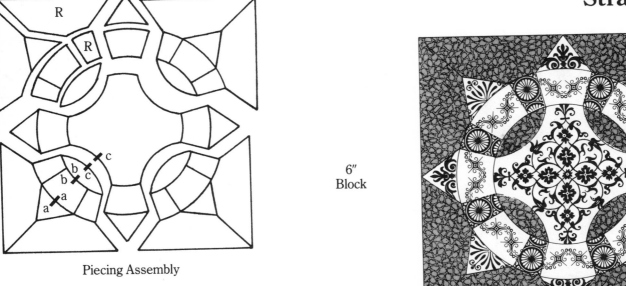

Piecing Assembly

Strawberry

6"
Block

Curved-Line Pattern

Mark all curved pieces with "joining marks" (A,B,C). This is very important to keep track of assembly. Put this block together as one major center part and four corner sections.

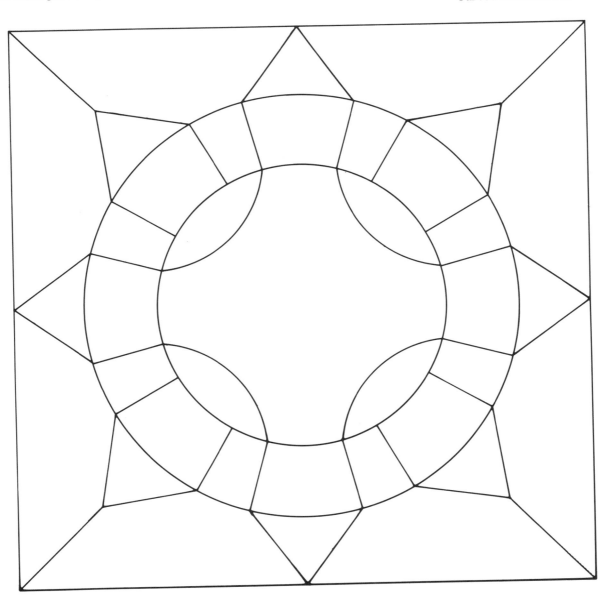

Mariner's Compass

Curved-Line Pattern

6"
Block

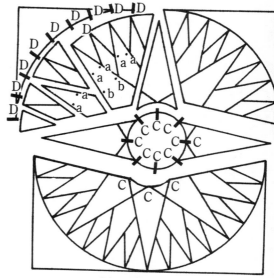

Piecing Assembly

Mark curved corner pieces and center circle with "joining marks" (D,C), and cone-shaped pieces with "joining marks" (A,B). Join smallest cones to next-size cone. Join these "pie shaped" wedges to each side of the next-size cone. Continue until there are two equal sections and a middle section. Join.

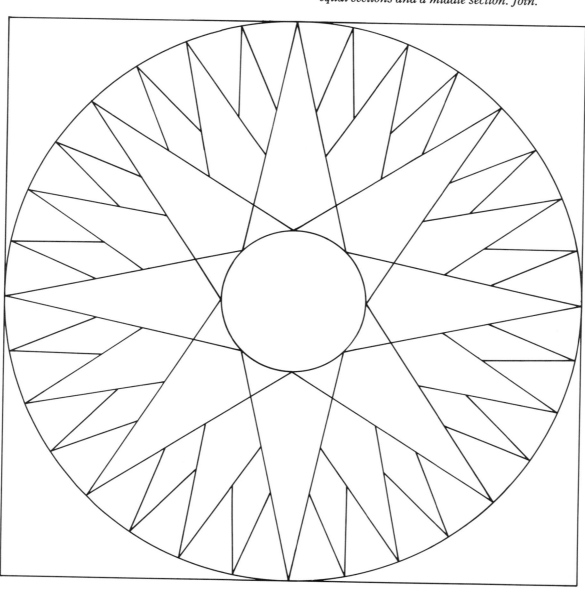

Mariner's Compass (Variation)

6″
Block

Piecing Assembly

Mark all curved pieces with "joining marks" (C,D,E), cone-shaped pieces with "joining marks" (A,B). Join the smallest cones to next-size cones; join curved-edge triangle. Join this "pie-shaped" wedge to next-size cone. Continue until there are two equal sections and a middle section. Join.

Curved-Line Pattern

Quilting the Quilt

Signature

Since you are in charge of what your great-great grandchildren will take for "show and tell" at the tricentennial, **sign and date your quilt.** Your signature may be bold or subtle, but it should be permanent. Placement on the front is usually in a corner, or in the center, or in a featured block. The signature may be embroidery, cross stitching, or in the quilting stitches!

For those who do not feel comfortable with embroidery, try a straight running stitch or back stitch continuously. Write your name and date (printed or longhand) on a piece of paper the size that will fit the space you have allotted for your signature on the quilt top. When it looks right and fits the space, go over the signature on paper with a dark pencil or pen. Slip the paper under the proper place on the quilt top. Arrange it until you can see the signature through the fabric. Lightly trace (using dotted lines) the signature on the fabric.

Now sew along this outline using tiny, even, running stitches (same as your quilting stitches). The trick here is to begin at the end of your signature and work back towards the start. This way if there are problems, you have more room to work them out. You may use mercerized or quilting thread, or embroidery floss. The color of thread may match or accent.

If a more "solid" look to the writing is desired, use a continuous back stitch. Begin at the end of the traced signature and take a tiny, even back stitch. The next back stitch will end where the previous back stitch began, one stitch joining to the end of the previous one. This will make almost a continuous line of writing with no space showing between the stitches. Longhand, or script, writing looks especially well done this way.

Another alternative for a signature is to write the information on a piece of muslin with an indelible, permanent marker. Turn under the edges of the muslin and slip stitch it to the back of your quilt. This will look like a label on the back of your quilt. Or a piece of muslin may be taped to a page of typewriter paper and inserted into the typewriter. The information is typed on the muslin and the muslin label is sewed to the back of the quilt. This method is especially good for quilts with many makers, a long history, or a lengthy explanation.

Quilting Designs

Designs will show off your quilting and can be used to give some of the plainer or solid areas of the quilt more interest. Counterpane blocks may use all the same designs, alternating designs, or a different design in each block. On the following pages are some designs for six-inch blocks along with matching border or sashing designs.

Many quilting design stencils are available. Quilt shops usually carry a kit and plastic for making your own stencils from printed patterns. Use your preferred method for transferring the quilting designs to the quilt top. Be sure to mark the design as lightly as possible. A "dotted" or "dashed" marking line is much less visible after it is quilted.

If the quilting is going to follow a line or outline in the printed fabric, then marking is not necessary. Masking tape of ¼" width is handy for marking straight lines or grids. Quilt along the line marked by one edge of the tape. Or if a double line is needed, quilt along each side. Tape is removed and it leaves no trace. Short pieces of tape work best and may be reused several times.

Color of the Thread

The color of quilting thread is very important. One color may be used throughout the quilt, or you may change and use several colors. If the quilt is meant for a bed or throw, where the quilt will be turned back, I usually use one color. If the quilt is meant for a wall or art piece where the back will seldom if ever show, I change color of thread as needed.

From studying Amish quilts, I have learned the importance of using darker colored thread for quilting. The Amish use black quilting thread almost exclusively on their vibrant colored quilts and the quilting shows up beautifully. Where the thread crosses a red patch, it appears a deep dark red; where it crosses a blue patch, it appears a dark navy blue.

The "valley" created by quilting thread appears deeper when a darker thread is used. White and very light colored thread appear to lie more on the surface of the quilt. I prefer to use a natural or ecru color thread for quilting on solid white fabric. The quilted piece appears much more contoured or "sculpted." Instead of perfectly matching the color of quilting thread to the fabric, try a darker, deeper shade of the color.

Unless a quilt is to receive very hard use and be washed frequently, regular mercerized thread may be used for quilting. Mercerized thread has the advantage of coming in many more colors than labeled quilting thread. I do not use beeswax on the thread because the wax tends to cause batting fibers to stick to it. These batting fibers are pulled to the surface of the quilt and look like "bearding" or fuzz. Some "bearding" will occur, but the wax seems to make it worse.

Pressing
Put a towel on the ironing board and place the quilt top on it with the right side up. Carefully press the entire quilt top.

Backing
The back of the quilt should complement or blend well with the rest of the quilt. A solid color fabric or print may be used. The quilting will show up more on the solid color fabric. If you are unsure of your quilting stitches, you may wish to put a print on the back so the quilting will be less visible. A print also helps disguise the use of different colors of thread. A print that appears somewhere in the quilt is generally better than a completely different one.

Cut the quilt back at least 2″ larger on all sides than the quilt top. For larger quilts, two or more lengths of fabric must be sewed together to make the back wide enough. Seams should be pressed to one side, not open. The back should be pressed free of all wrinkles.

Batting
There are many excellent batting materials on the market today—polyester, cotton, cotton-polyester blend, and wool. The choice is up to the quiltmaker. I use different batting in different projects, and all seem to work out well. The 100% cotton batting is harder to sew through and requires closer quilting to hold it in place. Cut the batting at least 2″ larger on all sides than the quilt top.

Quilt Sandwich
While on vacation, I needed to put a quilt sandwich together so I could begin my quilting. There was no table or floor surface large enough to spread out the project for pinning and basting. So I used a wall, and I've been using the wall ever since.

Remove pictures and exposed nails from the wall. Tape (masking tape) or pin (push pins) the back to the wall. Smooth out all wrinkles as you pin all sides of the back to the wall. Shake loose the package of batting, and pin or tape it over the quilt back on the wall. Wrinkles will tend to smooth as soon as batting is hung from the top. As you pin all sides, continue to smooth out any wrinkles.

Pin the quilt top over the layers of batting and backing. Align the quilt-top center with the center of the backing. Pin the quilt top to the wall on all sides, again smoothing out all wrinkles as you go.

The quilt sandwich (backing, batting, quilt top) is now ready to be pinned through all three layers. Extra long pins with large white beaded heads work very well. Start pinning each side of the center and continue pinning out in all directions. Make sure you are pinning through all three layers. The pins should not be more than eight inches apart.

When your quilt sandwich is completely pinned, remove push pins to release the sandwich from the wall. It is now ready to be basted. Baste the quilt from the center out in all directions. The pins may be removed after the quilt is basted. Your quilt sandwich is now ready for quilting.

Quilting
Quilting is an acquired skill. You must learn and perfect this skill. A teacher may show you, but you must learn to quilt by doing it. Learn the fundamentals from beginner books and watching experienced quilters. Then try all the different ways until you find what works best for you.

Whether you do your quilting using a frame or hoop, or lap quilt, is up to you. Try them all and see which you like best. If your stitches are small and even, and your quilt lies flat (no bulges) and straight, then you are doing it right. But there is always room to learn, so keep watching and trying new things.

Many quilters are ashamed to admit that they "lap quilt" without using either a frame or a hoop. There is no need to be ashamed. The advantage to hoops and frames is that all layers of the quilt are held in tension so that bulges and gathering of underside are eliminated.

Extensive basting of the quilt sandwich will eliminate much of the shifting and folding-over of the under layers. When lap quilting, keeping the quilt straight with some tension on it can be achieved by quilting at a table with the quilt spread out and over the table. Dressmakers' sewing weights (or heavy books) are placed on the quilt to hold it in place as you quilt. So it is okay to lap quilt and admit it!

Edge Finish
The edge of the quilt may be finished in one of several ways. First, trim any excess batting. The back may be brought over the front for a narrow width, turned under and the edge sewed down. With planning (the top must be larger than the back), the top may be taken over the back, turned under and sewed down. If the quilt edge is not scalloped or curved, a separate straight binding may be used on the edge. Scallops or curves along the quilt edge require that a bias binding be used to finish the quilt edge.

Diana Leone, in *Sampler Quilt*, gives excellent directions for making continuous bias binding strips.

Finis
One of life's real joys is when you can finally say, "I have finished my quilt."

1½" Border

Tiffany

Original Design
Libby Lehman
© 1983

Quilting Designs

Rondolet

Original Design
Libby Lehman
© 1983

1½″ Border

Georgian

Original Design
Libby Lehman
© 1983

Solar

1¾″ Border

riginal Design
ibby Lehman
1983

1″ Border

Essence

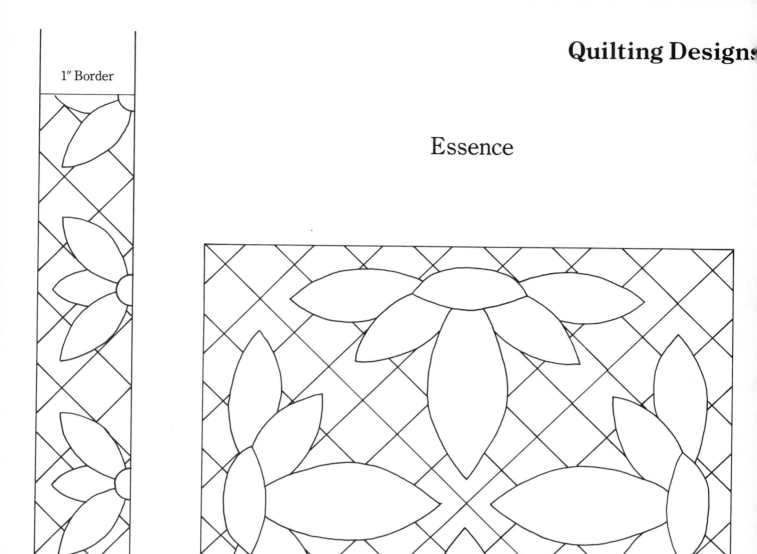

Quilting Designs

Garland

2″ Border

Original Design
Libby Lehman
© 1983

Bibliography

Beyer, Jinny, *Patchwork Patterns*, EPM Publications, Virginia, 1979.

Beyer, Jinny, *Quilter's Album of Blocks and Borders*, EPM Publications, Virginia, 1980.

Beyer, Jinny, *Medallion Quilts*, EPM Publications, Virginia, 1982.

Gutcheon, Beth, *The Perfect Patchwork Primer*, Penguin Books, N.Y., 1973.

Gutcheon, Jeffrey, *Diamond Patchwork*, Alchemy Press, N.Y., 1982.

Holstein, Jonathan, *The Pieced Quilt, an American Design Tradition*, New York Graphic Society Ltd., 1973.

James, Michael, *The Quiltmaker's Handbook*, Prentice-Hall, Inc., N.J., 1978.*

James, Michael, *The Second Quiltmaker's Handbook*, Prentice-Hall, Inc., N.J., 1980.*

Laury, Jean Ray, *Quilts and Coverlets*, Van Nostrand Reinhold, N.Y., 1970.

Leman, Bonnie, *Quick and Easy Quilting*, Hearthside Press Inc., N.Y., 1972.

Leman, Bonnie and Judy Martin, *Taking the Math Out of Making Patchwork Quilts*, MOM Publishing Co., Wheatridge, Colo., 1981.

Leone, Diana, *The Sampler Quilt*, Leone Publishing Co., Santa Clara, Calif., 1980.

Puckett, Marjorie and Gail Giberson, *Primarily Patchwork*, Cabin Craft, 1975.

Puckett, Marjorie, *Patchwork Possibilities*, Orange Patchwork Publishers, Orange, Calif., 1981.

Safford, Carlton L. and Robert Bishop, *American Quilts and Coverlets*, E. P. Dutton, N.Y. 1972.

*Reprinted by Leone Publishing Co., in 1993. Now distributed by Dover Publications, Inc., Mineola, N.Y.

About the Author

Catherine Anthony and quilting got together in 1972, and it has been an enduring friendship ever since. She found in the colors, patterns, and designs a creative outlet for artistic expression. Her quilts reflect a distinct personal style developed through intensive study and creation of original designs. Currently she is in the middle of making a series of quilts honoring women whose lives and contributions to society she respects and admires. There is little in common in this series other than creative and balanced design, impeccable workmanship, and an emotional response by those who see the works. As she developed her own style and methods, Catherine realized that teaching was another means of showing the love of quilting. She has taught, lectured, and judged around the country and internationally. She now owns a very well documented collection of Amish quilts which she shares in exhibits and lectures.

Catherine graduated with a B.A. degree from Rice University, majoring in biology and chemistry. She has been active in volunteer work in her church and the Girl Scouts. For twelve years she owned and operated The Quilt Patch, a retail quilting business in Houston, Texas. As a quilt appraiser certified by the American Quilting Association, she continues to show her knowledge and skills of quilts and quilting. She and her husband Jim have four daughters, six grandchildren, and one great-grandchild. They also share a love of the Southwest, theater, the arts, and travel.